A Million Suns

Advance Praise for *A Million Suns*

"*A Million Suns* leaves you with…a sense of happiness and attitude that we can overcome any obstacle. As Christopher Reeve once said, "nothing is impossible."

Peter Wilderotter, President and CEO,
Christopher & Dana Reeve Foundation

"*A Million Suns* is a compelling story of Kristin overcoming insurmountable odds with dignity, humor and grace."

Sheila Grant, athletic trainer and forever friend

"*A Million Suns* is an electrifying story of how determination and a positive attitude can help you overcome any challenge. Kristin gives you an inside look into the world of disability that will make you laugh, cry, and reevaluate your life."

Hunter Leemon, Executive Director of Sportable

"*A Million Suns* gives you a new perspective on what it means to be differently abled. It'll take you through highs and lows, and have you reconsidering your own life the whole while."

Roll with Cole & Charisma

"Kristin Beale, author of *A Million Suns*, is a fencer of exceptional promise for success in national and international competition; one of the best I have trained in my 52 years in the sport."

Walter G. Green III, Ph.D., Maitre d'Armes

"*A Million Suns* reminds me to live beyond my circumstances by living for today. Kristin's forward-thinking can only come when we stop trying to fix our past and learn to carry the reality of our story with authenticity, positivity, and courage. This book beautifully articulates a hopeful story through her hope-filled writing."

Stephen Poore, Pastor of Center Church

A
Million
Suns

Kristin Beale

NEW YORK

LONDON • NASHVILLE • MELBOURNE • VANCOUVER

A Million Suns

Published in New York, New York, by Morgan James Publishing. Morgan James is a trademark of Morgan James, LLC. www.MorganJamesPublishing.com

ISBN 978-1-63195-070-4 paperback
ISBN 978-1-63195-071-1 eBook
Library of Congress Control Number: 2020903410

Cover Design by:
Kacey J. Vaughn

Morgan James is a proud partner of Habitat for Humanity Peninsula and Greater Williamsburg. Partners in building since 2006.

Get involved today! Visit
www.MorganJamesBuilds.com

Table of Contents

Acknowledgments

Thank you to my whole family for supporting me. That includes my parents, sister Jessica, brother-in-law Tyler, boyfriend Chris, and my friends who have become my family. I'd be weird and unhappy without you guys.

Thank you to my team at Morgan James Publishing for making my dream come true over, and over, and over.

Thank you to everyone who supported and worked with me throughout these stories. My disability has become one of my favorite things about myself, and I couldn't have done that alone.

Thank you, thank you, thank you.

A Million Suns

E veryone learns from a young age that we can't have life without the Sun. Among a long list of benefits, sunlight gives us the ability to sustain life; without it, there would be no plants, animals, or people. Really, there's no such thing as life without Sun.

Every person on Earth lives under the same Sun, but no person's life is the same; the decisions we make and the lives we lead are all different. Because of the different directions our lives go, we perceive everything, even the Sun, differently.

Just like there are a million different stars, there are a million different suns.

Sun shines in everybody's life differently: sometimes bright, sometimes muted, sometimes direct and hot, and sometimes blocked by clouds. Every person is impacted differently by their sun; we're all dealing with something. We can either choose to put on sunglasses and embrace the sunlight, or stay in the shade and hide. We can choose to acknowledge that life isn't always good and we have to put in the effort to make it better, or we can accept our situation and just tolerate.

In my case, more than 15 years ago, life took seemingly everything away from me; I was in an accident that took some mobility and a majority of my sensation. It also caused me to lose friends, opportunities, and the life I imagined for myself. My sun had a cloud in front of it that I thought was going to be there forever. I was in the darkness.

I now realize there was value in my time in the darkness, though, because I used it to acknowledge my difference and adapt to my new circumstance. My darkness concentrated in high school and college and it brought on some loneliness and some tears, but I eventually reached a point of acceptance for myself. With that new perspective, I was able to step out of the darkness and eventually discover a happiness that I never, ever expected.

No matter the circumstances of your life, do whatever it takes to have a healthy mind about your situation. We all have uphill battles to climb, but the only way to survive is to live outside of the darkness and in the warmth of the Sun.

The Darkness

In the years leading up to being a teenager, my life was a basic, happy one. I had a full and loving family that included my mom, dad, and sister, Jessica; a group of friends to surround me; and I lived in a middle-class neighborhood in the suburbs. My story wasn't a particularly interesting one until the summer of 2005. More specifically, August of 2005 while I was on vacation with my friends in Lake Gaston, North Carolina.

Aubrey, the organizer of the weekend, is a friend I've had since elementary school. She went to my church and we were friends via church youth group, but we had only just started to hang out. At a church trip to Kings Dominion the weekend before, she introduced me to Feild, and I developed a pretty giant crush on him by the end of the day. Feild had a smile that melted me; a sense of humor that made me not want to be

3

away from him, with fear I would miss something; and he was handsome. He flirted with me in the way that made my face hurt from an unbroken smile.

Mark, the last character in this story, was a new friend; I only vaguely recognized him from the hallways of school.

The weekend was non-stop fun and I, being on my best behavior with a plan of making Feild like me as much as I him, was loving it. We swan in the lake, jumped off the roof of the boathouse, and I flirted my heart out. But, you know, in a cool way. I was playing it cool.

The rest of the information about the weekend I only know from what people told me; short term memory loss erased it all. It's strange to hear a retelling of something I lived through and have no recollection of, but that's all I have. I remember a few insignificant details of the weekend, but they're very insignificant and literally only a few. The rest is black.

Here's what I know:

On the last day of the weekend and the end of summer before our sophomore year of high school, the four of us split onto two Jet Skis: Feild driving Aubrey and Mark driving me. Combination of driver inattention and a No Wake Zone resulted in a collision that killed Mark and left me unconscious and bobbing in the water next to him.

The details of the accident, which we learned later on, are as follows: Feild, driving Aubrey, wasn't paying attention to the water ahead of him and slammed into and on top of my and Mark's ski. I was in the middle of turning around to see them approaching, and their ski hit me on the left side of my head and in the middle of my back. Mark wasn't as lucky. He was hit on the back of the head, fell forward into the steering wheel, and died on impact.

Now you see the context of my word "interesting." There was nothing flashy about this accident—until later on, at least.

We both fell in the water and a nearby boat saw it all happen. They were able to call the coast guard, who were minutes away, and get us out of the water in what I credit as record time. From the shore, we were loaded onto an ambulance and rushed to Halifax Hospital, where Mark was declared dead on arrival and my doctors said I wasn't far behind him. The Jet Ski's slam into my head gave me a traumatic brain injury with short term memory loss; my spinal cord was stretched at T8, resulting in paraplegia; I was unable to breathe on my own; I had water floating in my lungs; and there was a problem with nearly every one of my internal organs. I'll spare you my full list of injuries here, but trust me: it's exhaustive.

From Halifax Hospital, I was airlifted to the nearest trauma center, which was Pitt Memorial Hospital in Greenville, North Carolina. My parents and sister, Jessica, were told I would not live beyond those initial moments, but I was hanging on. I'm a fighter, and that was only the beginning of my fight.

It's impossible for me to fathom how much pain my family must have felt at that time and I can only believe they got their strength directly from God. My family was and has been solid as rocks through my initial and ongoing struggle.

I digress.

It took several weeks and many sleepless nights for my family but, gradually, things began to improve enough for me to be moved closer to my home: the trauma center at VCU

Medical Hospital in Richmond, Virginia. I was stable enough to make that move, yes, but only by a little bit. I spent about one month at VCU before I was, again, able to be transferred. Barely. My family packed up their comatose little girl and moved to Children's Hospital, also in Richmond. Granted, I was being moved to the critical care unit of Children's, but that's still a tiny bit more promising than the trauma unit at VCU.

My progress since first coming to the hospital, albeit limited, made my doctors change their forecasting to my family. I would live, they said, but I would be dependent on a feeding tube to eat, I'd be hooked to a ventilator to breathe, I wouldn't be able to feel or move below my injury level, talk, utilize the whole right side of my body, or comprehend the world around me. Basically, a veggie.

Contrary to what was "supposed to happen," I came out of my coma in mid-October, two months after the accident, and slowly began to disprove those predictions. At least it felt slow.

My short term memory loss stuck around for long enough to erase memories of the whole time I was dependent on breathing and feeding tubes, the surgeries required to repair my broken spine, my coming out of the coma, and the first moments after being told I will not walk or play sports again.

I do, however, remember things like those miserable inpatient PT workouts to strengthen the right side of my body (extra weak due to my brain injury); learning how to transfer from the floor and roll my wheelchair through the grass (a huge struggle for my atrophied muscles); and the hospital cafeteria food (you never get used to it). I attest that the only way I kept my sanity through those three months of being inpatient is my mother, who slept in an armchair next to my bed every night; my dad and sister, who came to see us every chance they got; and a regular flow of friends visiting me every single day until my release. That, and the steady stream of milkshakes from visitors, which were the only things I would eat.

I was discharged in mid-December of the same year. I had the fortune of being surrounded by my beautiful family and an incredible number of people from my community who came out to support and love on me. When I moved out of the hospital room, I came home to a loaner hospital bed stuck in my dad's office, and a house under construction to make it more accessible for me.

I also left that place with an improving memory, an only slightly weaker right side, and the skills to navigate the world in a wheelchair. Most importantly, though, I left with a new purpose for my life: share my story and regain feeling/movement in my lower body. I so, so badly want those doctors to be wrong about my prognosis.

As evidence of the stories in this book, I'm fully enjoying myself until I get to that point. There is no doubt in my mind that I'll learn to walk again but, in the meantime, I'm doing my best to have fun while I'm stuck in this wheelchair. That's the "happiness that came later on" I alluded to. The accessibility and mindset of the world can use some serious improvement, but my situation could be worse. That's sometimes the only thing that keeps me going: it could always be a lot worse.

Since my accident more than 15 years ago, I've grown up, my attitude has evolved, and I've moved on from most of the trauma of my accident. Now, I'm in pursuit of acceptance and contentment within this disability; I've been searching for a replacement for the passions I lost with my paralysis. Most aggressive of that loss is my ability to play sports with my peers. Adaptive sports, which I discovered shortly after getting out of the hospital, have been my key to "normalcy," whatever that means.

A rule I follow closely is to try new things at every opportunity I'm given. I'm driven not only by my curiosity and sense of adventure, but also by my search of something to make me feel whole again, not so "disabled." In an effort to fill the void that came with my paralysis, I've tried almost literally every sport available to me in its adaptive form. As result, I've found my passion in handcycling and fencing, and I've found the love of my life.

The lesson here is: regardless of the hills you have to climb to get to fulfillment, the pursuit is worth it one hundred times over. Whether disabled or not, we all need to find things to fill us up and let us live, as opposed to just exist. Everyone needs to find a way to move from the darkness, into the sunshine.

Exoskeleton

T he opportunity to be on my feet is something I'll never again take for granted. Before I was injured, my morning routine was to pop out of bed to my feet; walk to the bathroom and run a brush through my hair; slide into a pair of pants; and be ready to walk out the door in under twenty minutes. Blame that on my mascara-only beauty routine or, more relevant, my able body. Like most things, I didn't realize how good I had it until I lost it.

So now, after my accident, I have to find creative ways to get back upright. And here we come to the exoskeleton.

Nicholas, a friend from my sports team, posted a picture on Facebook of him standing tall in exoskeleton braces at a local rehab hospital. He's a quadriplegic and standing up was a humongous deal for him, so I wanted in on the fun. I don't remember how soon it was after seeing his post that I had an appointment of my own but, knowing me, it was within the hour.

————

"Okay," Amber said and looked up from the fastenings of my leg, which hung over the side of a table in the middle of the gym. "I'm ready when you are."

My face lit up in the way it does when ice cream touches sensitive front teeth, or when walking into the room of a surprise party. One is painful and one is exciting, but you get my point.

"I'm ready," I said, trying to play cool. A change in perspective the best part about standing up in exoskeleton leg braces, and the process of doing it is the most fun. There are a number of advantages to me standing up such as weight-bearing on my bones, improved circulation, and just generally stretching out my limbs, but being eye level with someone taller than a toddler is really something.

The exoskeleton braces I was using are unique and kind of tricky to explain using only words; there's not really a comparison I can make, so you'll need your imagination. The closest I can relate is that wearing the braces feels like a robot has swallowed and has control of each of my legs. There's only a small amount of control I can have over leg-hungry robots, so this analogy is a good one; the exoskeleton, to a degree, has a mind of its own.

Putting the imagination piece aside for a moment, though, I'll share what's really going on.

Exoskeleton leg braces look like two thick, black poles that run along the length of my inner and outer legs, stretching from heel to upper thigh. Those poles are fastened into a hip piece, the nucleus of the braces, that's used to detect my intention of motion. The nucleus communicates with the leg poles to lift my foot, move it forward, and stomp it down again. When I'm fully suited up, I am a complex machine.

"Scoot closer to the edge of the mat," Amber said. She shuffled behind me to steady my hips. Without saying a word, another man, whom I later learned was called Brendon, stepped in front of us to make sure I didn't fling too far forward with my scoot or stand. It's like these guys have a sixth sense of where to be, what to do. I guess that's also called "being trained."

"All right" I declared, as if I have the final say in when I begin. I don't. For the most part, I do whatever the therapists tell me because they're the ones that have to turn the power on my legs and turn on my machine. The combination of being controlled by the therapist and by the actual braces meant there was only a tiny, inconsiderable space for my preferences. But, my butt was on the edge of the mat and I was ready to go. "Let's do it."

When able-bodied people stand up, they lean forward a bit. The exoskeleton attempts to recreate "natural" movement as much as possible so, the language of the braces is: when I'm ready to stand, I lean forward.

I leaned my chest way forward over my thighs and waited for the vibration from my hips, indicating detection from the nucleus. My body rumbled for a second or two, then propelled me into a perfectly upright standing position. Here, imagine a rocket launch.

The braces shoot me up into probably the best posture I've ever had, which is cool. They keep my knees locked and sturdy, and that's one less [very important and tricky] thing for me to worry about. I support myself with arm crutches, which just look like walking sticks, in each hand.

Then, the game changes.

It seems like Standing Up Air is a whole lot easier to breathe than Sitting Down Air. Maybe being nose and mouth-level with all the butts while I'm sitting down has something to do with it. When I'm standing up, my body is stretched out and my lungs are able to fill up completely, which feels better than you would imagine. My hair takes on the aroma of peppermint, the pudge in my belly disappears, and all the boys come to the yard.

Or, at least, that's what it seems.

When I'm standing tall, I feel beautiful and like everything in the world is right. It blows my mind that people get to do that all day, every day.

Another reason I love this standing routine is the immediacy of comparison: this is what it feels like to need a wheelchair, and this is what it feels like to be normal. I don't make a big deal about standing anymore because I don't love sentiment and I've been on my feet many times with leg braces since my accident, but the opportunity to stand up and look relatively normal while doing so is something I'll never again take for granted. I've just gotten good at keeping a neutral face about it.

I'm working so hard to be able to stand up and get those feelings on a more permanent basis.

"It's still a little cold to go outside," Amber said from behind me. She gave me a moment to collect myself and breathe Standing Up Air before we started. "Let's walk down the hallway next to the window." She pointed her finger from behind me. "Through this door and to the left."

With the aid of my robot legs and a crutch on each arm, I tilted my right hip forward one inch to communicate to the machine that I was ready to walk. The hip piece detected my tilt, vibrated for another second, and lifted my leg up to stomp back down five inches in front.

The whole process of walking, as mechanical as it is, sounds like a muffled version of machines in a construction yard. More relatable, the sound of the claw game at the movie theater that's filled with stuffed animals. I'm really good at that game. That mechanical crunching is also the sound of Kristin walking down the hallway.

I'm making this process sound very smooth and effortless, but only because I haven't yet mentioned my unstable, jiggly upper body. I'm not claiming to have zero abdomen and lower back muscles, but I do admit to having less than the average bear. Walking with robot legs requires me to use and engage every bit of muscle and control I do still have, and that's no small task.

"How's it going?" Amber asked after about twenty minutes of me silently walking in circles around the sterile hallways of the hospital's outpatient clinic.

"My hands hurt and my arms are burning," I said. "But not enough to sit down." I tried to maintain pep in my voice so she wouldn't think I was being sarcastic. I actually was very excited about those pains.

"Okay," she said. "Good. Take a turn down that hallway and we'll walk toward the gym." Her finger pointed down the long, marbled floor. The hallway is a short errand while rolling in a wheelchair, but a long undertaking when walking in braces. Bring it on.

By the time I robo-walked through the gym, toward my wheelchair, and next to the mat in the middle, my body was done. Muscle fatigue in a paralyzed body is an interesting concept because no one knows it's there until my body collapses, my toes stop wiggling, and/or my muscles stop activating. At the end of an hour of walking, though, it's a pretty safe bet that my body is in full Fatigue Mode.

On the contrary, an hour of walking around gives me mental energy, excitement, and all the good feelings. The elation of my mind just doesn't translate to my body; when my legs or hips give out, I'm forced to oblige. That's sometimes frustrating.

———

Again with trying to mimic "natural" movements, when able-bodied people sit down, they bend slightly forward to bend their knees and glide toward the surface below. When I intend to sit in exoskeleton braces, I recreate that forward lean.

I reached the mat and positioned myself standing tall with the backs of my knees pressed against it and my butt sticking out. Amber pushed a button on the brace's controls and, as a shout out to all those boys in the yard, I bent farther forward to stick my butt farther out. I held that position for three to four seconds until I felt the vibration from my hips.

Similar to the routine of standing up, those vibrations trigger a mechanical movement to bend my legs back to a 90-degree sitting position. The charm of standing up is reversed for sitting down—it's kind of a bummer.

Once I'm seated, the hip piece switches to Standby Mode, the robots take my legs out of their mouths, and they back away.

"Great job today," Amber said. Even though I feel like all those good feelings could give me the endurance to stand up and walk around forever, my body appreciates a break. Even my upper body, which I would like to convince you is made of pure steel and is unable to tire, needs a break sometimes. Sometimes.

"You walked for almost the whole hour today," she said and looked at the controls on my brace. "974 steps."

Walking that long and far is a leap and bound improvement from when I first started walking in braces back in high school. Then, I could only stand for 15 minutes at a time before either my body fatigued, or my lightheadedness forced me to sit. I never thought that would ever get easier. Of course, having the robo-legs helped.

"Thank you," I said with more enthusiasm than I expected. My voice was apparently the only part of me that could still show it. "The crutches aren't so bad anymore."

Arm crutches, previously Instruments of Torture, were starting to feel comfortable—as comfortable as a walking aid can be, I guess. I never (ever) thought I'd progress to a point where walking with a walker is solace, but I worked very hard and, now, walking with a walker is cake. That just meant it was time to move to the next level. Obviously. So, I searched through The Devil's toy box and came out with arm crutches. I'm being dramatic here, but only a little bit.

Exoskeleton leg braces, like I said, changed the game.

Those leg braces made using the crutches manageable; allowed my skinny legs to support the gravity of my upper body; and gave me a new, higher perspective on the world. Walking and standing in leg braces is great not only because of the core workout, but also because it allows me to actualize the idea of a Standing Kristin. The experience brings me closer, if only for an hour each week, to the reality of effortless walking. I'm not sure if I'll ever be able to walk without thinking so hard about it or using so much of my intention to take steps, but the exoskeleton legs give me a flicker of hope. These days, that tiny flicker is all I need.

There's only one catch: owning my own exoskeleton would cost me upwards of $80,000. Let's not give up hoping, though.

Tennis

"Have you ever played before?" a man in a collared shirt walked from behind me and asked. His shirt was official with an emblem that read "Wheelchair Tennis 2013" in block letters on his back, and I safely assumed I was talking to my coach. Also, across his chest was a picture of a large racket, and the shirt was neon green.

A neon shirt is bold enough for me to assume, also safely, that it was from a tournament or official event. The color of the shirt, alone, reflected the kind of confidence only a coach can have.

"I have," I said, feeling cool for that moment. I don't know why I said "yes," though; I've played tennis before, but that was over 15 years ago, and I only lasted one season. I should have said "no" so he wouldn't expect any knowledge or skill from me. That way, I might at least have had a chance at impressing him.

"Great," he said. "Then you know the rules and how the scoring works."

I nodded and showed him my biggest smile. My smile was acknowledgment that I heard the words coming out of his mouth, not that they were true. I remember how the scoring works, one of the easiest concepts of the game, but almost literally none of the rules. It can't be too complicated though, right?

Fortunately, my only goal of that practice, if achieved, is the only thing I needed to do to make it look like I at least kind of knew what I was doing: hit the ball. It didn't matter where I hit it and even if it went over the net—I just wanted to hit the ball. I'd deal with the other rules once I had that mastered.

Adaptive tennis is a sport I didn't think I would ever have an interest in, much less have the opportunity to play. I'm not really saying I had a change of heart, either. I was expertly persuaded—persuaded by a sport wheelchair.

A couple of months prior to the first tennis practice, I went to an adaptive sports expo put on by Sportable, a Richmond-local organization that provides sports teams for a community of people with disabilities. It took me a few years to realize their opportunity, but they've helped me put sports back into the center of my life, and that has been beneficial in more ways than ten.

The most important way sports have impacted me is the return of something I can work hard at and see the results of my work reflected in my performance and body's health. Also, there comes a boost in my confidence, my attraction, and my self-esteem. Especially in my post-injured life, if something makes me feel better about myself physically or mentally, I'll chase it. Sports hit that nail on the head.

At the expo, each adaptive sport had its own booth with a coach, some sort of demonstration or visual aid, and a signup sheet. It was like eBay in real life and, with my impulse, please believe this is a dangerous situation for me to be in. I zoomed around the gym, spoke to four people, signed up for all four of their corresponding sports teams, and was heading toward the food table when a man spoke from behind me.

"Have you ever tried adaptive tennis?" he asked.

In my head I screamed "NOPE. NOT INTERESTED. BYE." But I'm a polite girl and I don't know how to say "no" to things, so I smiled at him.

"I haven't," said my sweetest voice. "I'm not extremely interested, though."

That's fairly direct of me, so I was probably doing something sweet like rubbing his head while I attempted at rejection. You know, to soften the blow.

"Have you ever used a sport wheelchair?" he pressed on.

In my head, where I can be assertive, I shouted "YES I PLAYED LACROSSE IN ONE AND DIDN'T LIKE IT. NO THANKS. NEVER AGAIN."

But I'm polite, so I went with "I did once, but it was a long time ago" and a smile.

"Why don't you sit in that one and give it a spin?" he said and pointed to a wheelchair that, for some reason, was parked unattended in the middle of the gym floor.

"NO THANKS. TENNIS AND BASKETBALL ARE THE SPORTS I'M NOT INTERESTED IN TRYING. GOODBYE."

But, remember, I'm a "yes" girl.

"Okay thanks," I said. "I'll give it a try."

Then I transferred into the wheelchair, and everything changed.

A sport wheelchair, I estimate, weighs in at about twenty pounds with the wheels on. The wheels are slanted inward to allow me to whip around like a dreidel, and the backrest is about 50% shorter than my already extra-low wheelchair back. There are also no brakes. All those things combined make it 100% more likely for me to accidentally to fling my body out, flip it over backward, and acquire another brain injury.

But, anti-tippers.

Otherwise a further-crippling and somewhat nerdy-looking addition to manual wheelchairs, tiny anti-tipping wheels set on the ground behind me and lined up with the middle of the chair's back are essential to a sport wheelchair. Because the chair is so lightweight, one normal-strength push would send me flying and likely smack me hard on the ground. The extra low backrest doesn't do much to prevent my flapjack fall, either. You get the point.

None of that matters, though, because these sport wheelchairs had that extra anti-tipping wheel and, for that reason, they're the most fun.

I rolled around in the chair for about two minutes before returning to the table and signing up for the adaptive tennis team. At that point, I would sign up for whatever I needed to in order to get more playtime in that sport chair. Within reason, of course.

"Welcome to the team," the strange man said. "We're going to have fun this year."

"Yeah right," I thought. "I'm going to have fun because I'll be in that chair. The tennis part is the bummer."

I smiled and nodded my head. "See you in the Spring."

By the time I left the expo, tennis and lacrosse, surprising to me, were on my list of sports to try (and to try again). I've given lacrosse a chance in the past and have even said "I'll never play again," but see? I was persuaded. The power of a sport wheelchair is real.

————

The first tennis practice came, and with it my first exposure to the adaptive version of a sport I tried so long ago. I didn't like it when I played as a kid, but here's to second chances.

In the first ten minutes of practice, I learned a few things. First, carrying a tennis racket while maneuvering a wheelchair as quickly as possible around the court does not come naturally. Or easily, for that matter. I glided and coasted around the court, missing every ball that wasn't served directly to me. I finally paid attention to my peers enough to figure out not an easy approach, but an approach: include the racket's handle in my grip while pushing my wheelchair around the court. Somebody probably could have told me that and saved some time but that's how we learn, right? I guess.

The second lesson is that I was correct in my underestimation of my Tennis Memory. I knew I was supposed to serve the ball into the box opposite side of the net and the balls have to land inside the big box on the court, but that's about it. Thanks to my coach's foundationless confidence in me, though, he kept checking in and saying things like "Does that feel familiar to you?" and "Is that how you play it, Krista?"

I guess I didn't enunciate when I introduced myself.

I just nodded my head and said "Oh yeah. That's how I play." Somehow, that was good enough.

After everyone was assessed and shown the basic rules of forehand, backhand, and adjustments of the adaptive version (two bounces instead of one, wheels behind the baseline while serving, etc.), we split into groups of four to play a doubles match. I was paired with a girl who said she "has been playing tennis for six years," so I was a bit intimidated. But hey. If I wasn't good at it yet myself, an experienced doubles partner is the perfect situation.

Turns out, she wasn't any better than I was. I think the "six years" part was an exaggeration.

Our opponents were, very obviously, well beyond their first season of playing adaptive tennis. But I had a victory: my ball didn't make it over the net, but I managed to make ball-to-racket contact one time. One time! Like I said, my goal was to hit the ball, not necessarily hit it in the right direction. Those skills would come later. Hopefully.

When I did hit that ball, though, I felt cool for one more moment.

The rest of the practice was filled with me swatting at the air with my tennis racket and lots of forced laughter, but it was fun. I missed every ball after that first hit, but it was enough to get me to return next week.

That, and the attractive man in a wheelchair playing on the court next to mine.

————

"Pair up with a doubles partner," the coach yelled from the sideline. "We're going to work on your serves today."

This was the second practice and it felt like I had barely learned the sport, but they loved to throw us into those doubles matches. That's the best way to learn, I guess: try, mess up, correct. I rolled my chair forward to the baseline in front of me.

"Zoomed" is a better word than "rolled"—I zoomed forward to the baseline. I was in a sport chair, remember.

"Split up on the two sides of the court," the coach yelled again. Two familiar faces, my opponents, rolled to the opposite side of the court. "This side will serve first." He pointed to my side, thank God. "The other side will work on returns."

This was my victory because I like serving the ball. My preference speaks nothing to my skillset, but serving the ball to start the game granted me power, my only bit of power, to initiate gameplay. Also, serving the ball is great because I don't have to move around the court and fumble with holding a tennis racket while I roll.

"I'll stand behind you guys and give you balls to hit," a man stepped up and said to me and my nice-looking partner,

Grace. He wasn't just any ol' man, either. He was beautiful and young and wasn't wearing a wedding ring. "My name is Matt," he said and smiled, I would like to think directly at me.

"Matt," I thought. "You can give me balls to hit any day."

Instead of saying that, because I am a lady, I smiled my sweetest and said, "okay great."

He fed us balls, I hit them with the excuse I wish I had of with both of my eyes closed, and I stole glances at Matt whenever he looked away.

No surprise, I'm much better at serving tennis balls than returning the balls, which isn't saying much. Again, it's my strength mostly because I don't have to move around to do it. Matt's "nice shot" and "good serve" comments from behind made me believe so, at least.

Or, maybe he was just saying those things to flirt with me until he worked up the nerve to ask for my number and kiss me on the face. I can't be sure.

After a couple rounds of serving the balls and turning to my beautiful ball assistant to get more, I made a plan: serve the balls faster, visit him more often, train him like a rat. I learned this technique in Behavioral Psychology class: perform the same action-and-reward set for enough repetitions until the rat, Matt in this example, grows to expect it. If I saw results of anything like Pavlov's dog experiment, Matt's mouth will start salivating in anticipation of my coming.

I am the perfect mixture of an undergraduate Psychology scholar and an utterly single woman.

But, it actually did kind of work. Matt was giving me and Grace handfuls of three balls at a time whenever he saw we were out. Remember the trick: in the beginning, this was often because I was getting rid of my balls quickly. I slowed my pace and Matt, the little lab rat he is, kept delivering balls even though I clearly didn't need any more. I ought to get some kind of award for this.

You better believe I accepted every ball he offered to me, though, need it or not.

"Thank you," I said after each delivery. My gratitude was meant to reward his behavior within my experiment, yes, but also to give me an extra shot at eye contact.

All good things come to an end.

My serves, like I've already bragged, aren't so bad. The problem comes when I have to return the ball. Thankfully, in these practices, everyone is still learning the sport, so there aren't many serves that are returned. In the rare times I have to hit it back, though, I know exactly where I fall short: I serve the ball, realize I made a good hit, feel very happy, and I want to watch it bounce around on the other side.

What I should be doing and what I was trained to do, is back my wheelchair to the baseline and prepare for the potential return shot. I just get so happy and caught up in my victory that I completely miss the return. Ninety percent of the time, I miss the return. That's something I need Matt to give me a private lesson on, I guess.

"Everyone play your last ball," the coach yelled. "Then come meet me on the sideline."

I collected one last ball from Matt and tried my best to wink at him as I grabbed it. This probably just looked like a very hard blink. At this point he might think I have something wrong with my brain, as well as my legs.

"Thank you," I said, blinked hard, and turned toward the baseline. I served the ball directly into the net and released a loud, high pitched laugh. Maybe my laugh will make it look like that net-serve was deliberate. Let me hope.

"Good job today," the coach said once everyone had gathered in a circle around him. "We'll work on your fore-and-back hands next week. You guys can leave before it starts to rain."

I looked at the sky and noticed its charcoal color for the first time. I had been so caught up in my Adaptive Tennis Love Story that I hadn't noticed the impending downpour. I turned to give Matt one last hard blink, but he was already on the other court collecting balls. He was, and is, a beauty. Those balls he was collecting probably saved me from making a bigger fool of myself, though, so someone is looking out for me.

"Bye everyone," I shouted to the group of disabled athletes transferring back into their normal wheelchairs. I got a few small acknowledgments in return but everyone, like me, was distracted by leaving as quickly as possible to beat the rain. That's okay.

I slung my bag in my lap and hurried back to my car. After spending two hours in a sport chair, my light-as-possible everyday wheelchair felt heavy to push around. As if God was waiting for me to find shelter, the rain started to drop as soon as my wheelchair was loaded in the seat next to me and I shut my car door.

"See you next week, babe," I said out loud and alone in my car. I was talking to Matt but, once again, someone was looking out for me; the rain saved me from looking like a fool. I smiled and watched him for one more minute. It was creepy.

Horseback Riding

I rode a horse once in middle school, well over fifteen years ago, and I remember it well enough to have stayed away from horses into my adult life. My friend, whom I've since lost touch with, lived on a farm several miles outside of Richmond and invited me to ride one of her two horses after school one day. We had a great afternoon and nobody was trampled but, still, I walked away thinking "that was cool, but probably never again."

It's not that horses aren't majestic and extremely intelligent animals, it's that they're smelly, uncooperative to my tiny voice, and they poop with zero regard for their surroundings. It was an okay experience for one afternoon, but only because I could ride on the horse then drive away without worrying about cleanup or maintenance. It's kind of like being a grandmother, or a dinner guest.

Again with the second chances, I thought it would be worthwhile to give horseback riding another shot—as a disabled athlete this time. Over and over again, I've learned my lesson about the word "never."

––––––––

"How do you want to transfer?" Caroline asked. She was standing next to me on the landing of a metal ramp, looking back and forth between me and a large horse. The horse was standing still next to the landing and, so far, it was cooperative with human commands. But you never know. It's a horse. Literally, you never know.

"I can just transfer onto the saddle if someone helps swing my leg over," I said. "As long as the horse stays still, I can do that." My voice didn't give away any apprehension, but, see above.

"Okay," Caroline said. She looked to a man I hadn't noticed was standing on the ground opposite the horse. They smiled at each other with a small nod, as if they were speaking a secret language and I said a keyword. "Mike will grab your leg."

"Yeah," he confirmed. "Just tell me when."

The three of us stood there with a plan. My declaration that I can "just transfer onto the saddle" made me appear very well-practiced in horseback transfers; I likely came off a lot more confident than I felt. But I wasn't going to show that weakness—not this early on. This is a game.

"By the way, this is Ivy," Caroline said. "He's our smallest horse. Very well behaved. We've had a few people in the therapeutic program ride him already."

I know she said that to comfort me, but all it really did was give a name to the monster. It's not that I was scared to ride, just that I realize how easy it is for an animal of that size to trample on and murder my small body. I wasn't scared—just aware.

"Hey buddy," I very awkwardly looked at the horse and said. The only relation I could draw was to my dog, whom I talk to like a full-on human. "How's it going?"

The horse can't speak English, of course, so everyone was silent after my greeting. If I knew them better I would have laughed at myself to break the moment, but silence felt good in this case.

I filled the uncomfortable air by scooting to the edge of my wheelchair seat to stare at Ivy's big horse belly, as if I was thinking about something important. It was more of a distraction than anything else. The only thought in my head was "ooch."

The metal landing we were sitting and standing on was built specifically so that Ivy's back was level with the edge. Those level surfaces made for an almost-even transfer onto the saddle and less possibility for my wipeout, which I was grateful. Still, though, it's a horse.

"Here we go," Mike said, grabbed the ankle of my right foot, and guided it over the horse's body to the opposite side of the saddle. The level of comfort it took to just grab up my limbs like that—I love it. Mike and I reached that level quickly, which is an accomplishment in itself.

I put one hand on my chair's seat and one on the hard leather seat of the saddle and pushed up to slide two inches from where I sat. It was a surprisingly easy slide onto the horse. Compared to what I was expecting, it was very simple. I might have even gotten away with looking like I knew what in the world I was doing, which I certainly did not.

"Nicely done," Caroline nearly shouted at the both of us. "Hold on, Kristin, and I'll jump down there and teach you some commands."

I nodded my head and Mike stood faithfully beside me, holding a belt I just realized was around my waist. I'm not sure how they snuck that on without my noticing.

Caroline reappeared at the horse's side moments later. I was now surrounded by Mike on my right and Caroline on my left, which made me feel slightly more comfortable. The combination of my decreased abdomen muscles and a five-foot-tall horse means I'm never completely confident that I won't fall to my death.

There was, I have to mention, a small and hard handle at the front of the saddle for me to hold onto. I think it must have been a leather-wrapped brick, though, because my thumb muscles screamed in pain after only twenty minutes of holding on to it. I might have also had what Caroline called a "death grip," but I prefer to blame the handles. After all, this is my story.

"Are you ready to move?" Caroline asked. I nodded my head and smiled big, too big perhaps. She made a "yip" sound, grabbed a rope draped over the horse's neck, and walked forward very slowly. The horse, recognizing a signal to move, also started walking.

And my whole world became unsteady.

"You're doing great," Caroline shouted up to me. From where she stood, the top of her head was level with my hip.

"This is better than I thought," I said.

That was my secret way of saying: "I thought I was going to hate this and regret giving horseback riding another try, but I don't so far."

"It's also not as difficult as I thought," I added. My middle school memory was laden with a suffocating smell of poop, an animal mind that I couldn't read, and being tossed left and right with the horse's movements. This experience, so far, wasn't as dramatic. Either my memory is exaggerated, or those horses were very poorly trained, but we're going to assume the latter. Again, my story.

The four of us, three humans and a surprisingly cooperative horse, walked around a living-room-sized enclosure three more times. Somehow, and to my surprise, I remained on the saddle the whole time. Maybe I didn't give myself or the horse enough credit, but I thought I would have at least come close to a fall by now.

"Okay," Caroline beamed up to me. "If you're comfortable, we can try walking over those poles." I had noticed the thick, plastic poles lined on the dirt, but I didn't realize they were there for a purpose. My face must have given away some of that confusion because she added "when Ivy walks over them, it feels a little different. She'll still be walking slowly."

That last reassurance was not necessary. I was ready, am always ready, to level up.

"Let's do it," I said. This time, I didn't say much beyond that, so I wouldn't have to play the Fake Confidence Game again.

Caroline smiled at me and redirected Ivy toward the middle of the enclosure with a small tug at his rope. We arrived at the poles in maybe five seconds time. Remember: living-room-size enclosure.

"Okay. I'm going to walk him over the poles when you say you're ready," she said. "I don't think you'll have a problem with this."

I nodded my head and the three of us started forward over four strategically placed poles on the ground. For me, the feeling of the horse stepping over the poles was minimally-to-not-any different than the feel of his normal walking. I don't see what all the fuss was about.

Walking over plastic poles is like switching from ice cream to frozen yogurt: you can tell something changed, but it's small enough of a difference to not be bothered.

"Woah," Caroline said to the horse and he obediently slowed down. We walked over two sets of poles two times each before stopping. Then, Caroline turned and looked up at me. "We have twenty minutes left. Do you want to learn to steer?"

"Yes," I said with a smile. Always ready to level up.

"I don't usually teach this on the first lesson," she said. "but you're doing great. I think you're ready."

My butt was still on the saddle, so I had a feeling I was doing an okay job. It's pretty exciting to hear the word "great" to describe my first ride in so many years, though. Weird, and I never thought I'd say it, but horseback riding was kind of fun.

"Okay," Caroline started. "Take this rope in each hand. Put your thumb on top of your grip and pull the rope toward the way you want Ivy to turn."

I took the rope from her hands and pulled on it like I was trying to steer an earthworm. I was dealing with an animal stronger than anything I've ever even come close to having power over, so it seemed reasonable to be gentle when yanking on his head with a dirty rope.

"You have to nudge him a little harder than that," she corrected and took the rope from me. She yanked on it once and Ivy's nose whipped to the left. She was being more aggressive than I would have but, on the contrary, a horse is the strongest animal I've ever touched. Some aggression is apparently necessary. Ivy immediately changed direction and headed toward the left.

"Think about pulling your hand toward your hip," Caroline instructed. She handed the rope back to me, I quickly accepted it with my left hand, and resumed my grip to the leather-wrapped brick. Maybe with time I'll feel comfortable enough to not grip with Satan's fury but, for now, white knuckles.

While steering Ivy, I could only hold onto the handle with my pinky fingers so I would be able to hold the rope with each thumb on top. I had to prioritize and, so far so good, the ropes took precedence. As instructed, I pulled my right hand and rope back toward my right hip. The horse made a dramatic turn to the right. With that, Mike said his first words since I started riding: "great."

With me in control and armed with the knowledge of how to steer the monster, we wove between cones, walked diagonally across the enclosure, and along the bordering fence. It was uncomfortable because I was on the back of a large horse, but comfortable because I was getting the hang of it. If that makes sense.

"How do you feel?" Caroline asked after no more than ten minutes of my directed swerves. "Our time is almost up."

"I feel great," I said. "My hands feel like they'll explode, but other than that I feel great."

I managed to settle into the ride enough to loosen my grip on the brick handle a tiny bit, but I was still holding way too tightly. Yes—it was painful. It was less pain than the alternative of a brain injury from falling to the ground though, am I right?

"You'll be sore tomorrow morning," Caroline promised. "Your core is working hard."

"I hope so," I said. Her head whipped around to me so dramatically. "I love being sore."

"That's strange," she said. She didn't smile when she said that, either. In my mind, I applauded our relationship for so quickly reaching the point of comfortable judgment.

Ivy arrived in front of the metal landing and stopped walking. It was either very impressive for him to know where to go without being told, or very crafty of Mike to give him a command without me hearing.

"This is the fun part," Caroline said. We hadn't quite reached the landing, so I wasn't super clear on the dismount plan. It was also unclear whether "fun" was sarcastic, or if I really was in for a good time. "It's easier for us to unload you onto the ground, instead of to the ramp." She turned to Mike. "Will you grab her wheelchair?"

He nodded and zipped up the ramp toward my chair. My wheelchair-to-horse transfer was simple, but a horse-to-wheelchair transfer is daunting, to say the least. Especially because, lest we forget, it involved a five-foot drop.

"You're going to move your leg to this side," Caroline said from the ground below. "Then slide yourself into my arms so we can put you back in your wheelchair."

"This is good," I said. I was both confirming to them and trying to convince myself. "Okay. I'll bring my leg over."

I lifted my right leg to swing over the horse's back and saddle. My balance surprised me; I was able to sit for this transition without falling off. I'm not sure how impressive that sounds, but it was a pretty big deal when you compare to my expectations.

The same second both my legs were next to each other, Caroline and Mike clung to my body and eased me down. We were working together in a way that seemed like we had done this many times before, which was cool. As emphasis from my initial transfer, it's a great feeling to achieve something on the first attempt, and look smooth doing it.

Once they plopped me in my seat, all three of us stood there and smiled at each other for a couple of seconds.

"That was a great ride," Caroline confirmed. Silent Mike nodded his head and either mumbled "yes" or made a complicated grunt. "You're a natural."

"I really enjoyed it," I said, genuinely. It felt like an overstatement to call me a "natural," but I definitely wasn't going to argue the point. "I like this."

Caroline took the saddle from Ivy's back, unhooked a few straps from his neck, and let Mike lead him back to the barn.

"Do you want to ride again next Friday?" she asked. In my head it almost sounded like she was pleading me to have another lesson, but maybe that's just my ego. Or maybe not, ya know?

"Yes," I said. "Yes, definitely. Put me on your schedule for every week."

She walked next to me out of the enclosure, away from the small farmhouse, and toward my car.

"I'll text you about times," Caroline said. She stopped walking when we reached my car, which was parked next to a huge tree. "Have a good weekend." She smiled and turned toward the barn.

"See you on Friday," I said with a smile, still very genuine. Horseback riding is an unexpected sport for me (see: middle school declaration of "never again"), but I was giving it a fair chance—eight weeks seems like a pretty fair chance. I wasn't *in love* with it yet but, if at the end I still haven't fallen and found the passion I'm searching for, onto the next sport.

I loaded myself and my wheelchair into the car and sat for a moment, watching Ivy walking slowly into the barn ahead of me. I think I should have felt tired from the "workout," but I didn't at all. I looked forward to the morning, though, when Caroline said my muscles would be sore.

When I woke up the next morning, my body felt great.

Modeling

"What is all this stuff?" I asked under my breath and parked my wheelchair in front of a wide mirror on the wall. Kelly didn't hear me, I don't think, because she didn't respond. Either that, or she was saving herself from explaining to me all the items on the makeup table that stretched the length of the room.

When I say, "on the makeup table," I really mean "completely covering the makeup table." As this was my first experience in the modeling industry, every brush, sponge, and product in the room was curious. It's probably best that I was ignored.

"All right sweetie," she stood in front of me and said. I managed a "yes" through my teeth because she was not just looking, but staring, at my face. I assume this is some kind of makeup trick to pick up on facial tones and textures so she could choose the right shades, but I was just saying a "thank you" prayer in my head for not having a breakout that day. That would have been sad.

"Is this your first time modeling?" Kelly started small talk while she searched for, grabbed, and put aside tools and palettes that were also foreign.

"It is," I said.

That was only partially true, though, because Jessica and I completed a modeling program in middle school. It was great because we learned how to apply makeup, a skill I have absolutely forgotten, and how to walk down the runway at a fashion show, which I'm no longer able, but it never amounted to anything; I got interested in sports and Jessica started musical theater, so modeling took a back seat.

Actually, we kept the program a secret from everyone, saying we were going to "an appointment in the city" once a month. Me personally, I didn't tell anyone because I didn't want people to think "Kristin is a model? She's not attractive enough for that," or even just "haha" at me.

Childhood insecurities, ya know?

Now, as a shout out my middle school version, Mom and I were on a road trip to Washington, DC for round two.

"Well, this is a lot of fun," Kelly assured me. "You're going to like it." Meanwhile, her hands were moving at 10mph around my head: blotting brushes in brown dust, squirting nude-colored cream on a Q Tip, hovering a palette of eye shadow next to my temple, and dotting the top of her hand with different color lipsticks. My face was a canvas, quite literally.

Knowing that I'll likely not have the opportunity to be face-painted like this again, I was enjoying myself very much. Normal Everyday Kristin only wears mascara. If I'm feeling fancy or attending a very special event, I'll swipe my eyelid with a purple eyeliner I've had since high school, but that hasn't happened in I don't know how long. My lack of effort either comes from confidence in my natural appearance, or complete laziness to the process, and it's very likely the former. Also, like I said, I forgot everything I learned.

Few minutes of conversation and I found out Kelly was in a car accident in her youth and also had a traumatic brain injury, so we swapped stories and bonded over that. A side effect of visible disability is people feel the need to overshare to find common ground with their (or their loved one's) traumatic situations. That's wonderful and I love it because I'm made privy to other people's business, but it's a little bit of a bummer way to bond. Really, though, anything that results in connection or friendship is fine with me. My disability certainly makes life more interesting.

"Okay, girl," Kelly said after about 25-30 minutes of face painting. "I think you're good, but go get your hair done, then ask Patrick if he wants something different."

"Okay," I said. I wouldn't be too bummed if he wanted something different because having my makeup done is fun and I enjoyed conversation with Kelly. But c'mon.

"The hair room is next door," she said and pointed her colorful hand at the doorway.

"Thank you," I said and winked a darkened eyelid at her.

Something you should know: I don't know how to wink. My attempt looks like hanging my mouth open and forcibly blinking both eyes, sometimes with a head tilt for extra effect. Despite how I know I look, I still try it sometimes. Kelly, like Matt my tennis coach, probably saw my effort and thought I still have a brain injury.

I took a last glance in the mirror before leaving the makeup room, but it was set high on the wall so I could only see the top of my forehead. I only saw a small portion of my face, but it was bronzed and even-toned, at least.

I rolled into the next room and stopped next to a couch with two other girls waiting their turn. One of them had beautiful and flowing hair already, so maybe she already had her turn. In my mind, a model is an entirely different and superior brand of person. So, also, maybe she woke up like that.

"I can take you after I'm done with her," the lady standing next to the swivel chair said. "My name is Lisa," she said quickly, distracted. "I'm doing everyone's hair."

I smiled, nodded my head, and saw she was doing what looked like finishing touches on another beautiful girl. Like Kelly, her station was set in front of a table covered in tubes and jars. Who knew there are that many different things to put on hair?

"Who is your agent?" one of the beauties on the couch asked me. This was probably go-to small talk for all the other girls but, they didn't know yet, I was a fish out of water.

"I don't have an agent," I said. "A friend forwarded me an email saying they were looking for 'women with visible disability,' and I took it." Again, thank you disability. "How long have you been modeling?"

"I've been modeling for three years."

The second girl on the couch looked up, so I raised my eyebrows at her to mean "what about you?" so she would join our conversation. I'll probably never see those girls again, but I wanted them in my corner. The second girl was the one with the naturally beautiful hair, and it made me want to touch it. If I'm nice enough to and include her, she might let me touch it. Creepy? Yes.

"About two years," she said. I nodded my head to both of them because I didn't really know what else to do. Thankfully, it was my turn before I got awkward.

"I'm ready for ya," she said and locked eyes with me. She was wiping her hands on a towel, some mystery cream from those tubes and jars. "Pull up to the mirror and I'll move this chair out of your way." She lifted the swivel seat from the ground and relocated it behind her.

This, I knew, was going to be the best part. Back massages are wonderful and hand massages are great but, when someone plays with your hair, it's a different ball game.

"You have great hair," she said and ran one hand through it, marking the beginning of the massage. I braked my wheelchair in front of her product table. "Thick."

"Thank you," I said with a smile. After a minor surgery the year before, my hair started falling out by the handful and to the point I feared people would notice. Post Medical Procedure Hair Loss is, without question, more traumatizing than surgery itself. Thank you, God, for giving me my father's thick hair genes.

"I'm not going to do much to it," she said. "Just some mousse and shine."

She held up two bottles, one I recognized as the mousse Mom used to chase us around with when we were young kids. The way Mom tells the story, Jessica and I ran through the house screaming "*NOT THE MOUSSE*" with our naked hinneys and not a thought of modesty.

The other, "shine," looked like a quarter-sized squirt of suntan lotion that she rubbed into her hands and quickly streaked through my hair. I didn't see it make a difference but, similar to the makeup situation, all I do to my hair at home is blow-dry and spot straighten when my waves get unruly. Do your thing, Lisa.

"That should be good," she said and patted the top of my head like a dog. "Head on over to the green room and they'll tell you what to do next."

"Thank you," I said and glanced toward her table of products. Again with the high mirrors, I could only see my forehead and side-parted hair. But my part was shiny, kind of?

I navigated out of the room into a hallway of doors— behind only one of them was the green room I was supposed to go have my pictures taken. I didn't see any other models standing around in the hall, so I guess "head on over" actually means "go quickly."

"Great," Patrick's voice sang from behind one of the doors. I was headed in the complete opposite direction, so his voice clue was helpful. I followed the voice and opened that door only enough to fit my chair through, and parked in the back of the room. "Hold that pose."

A new girl was standing on a black mat with a green sheet behind her, presumably for the cameras to add in background later. The "great" pose she was holding was a slightly bent right leg, left hand softly touching her hip, and head tilted one inch to the left. She was smiling at the camera, and her long hair fell to her middle back.

My wheelchair-bound body type is so completely different from these girls. Two trains of thought: "I don't fit in and I'm uncomfortable," or "my look is unique and therefore valuable." I'm sticking with the latter.

I had similar feelings in my middle school modeling experience, but they were a little different. Back then, the insecurities sounded like: "these people don't have chub under their chin like I do" and "they can walk down a runway without tripping." I don't have those same concerns anymore, but it just goes to show that, if you nitpick, there will always be something you won't like. It's exhausting. Everyone, stop nitpicking.

"Okay, let's take video," Patrick directed. Everyone in the room moved to obey: the man with the camera switched his equipment, another man readjusted the spotlights, and the girl unfroze her body back to the center of the mat. The transition was very smooth, presumably from years of practice.

"Look straight at the camera and say, 'Be the One,'" Patrick said to the girl. She nodded her head once and launched into it, saying "Be the One" over and over—about twenty times. Her delivery varied slightly with every repetition: sometimes she cocked her head to the left; sometimes more emphasis on "Be" and sometimes on "One;" sometimes her hair was in front of her shoulder versus behind; and every other seemingly meaningless detail you can think of. I don't know how she felt, but it made me feel silly just watching. She was doing exactly the right thing and was well-practiced in this business, though, so my feelings were definitely unnecessary.

Patrick gave the girl two more phrases and she repeated them to the camera twenty more times. She gave the same variation of head tilts, word emphasis, and hair placement while Patrick and the video crew looked on. It was all very exciting. Now that I had my face painted and hair poofed, I was excited for my turn in the spotlight.

"Thank you," Patrick said to the girl as she stepped off the black mat. "Very nice." He turned his body to look in my direction. "Are you ready?"

I was. I nodded my head and rolled toward the black mat. Every move with my made-up face and volumized hair felt like a statement, and I was confident. Is that how people feel when they wear makeup every day? Is that why they wear makeup every day? Makes you think.

"Park yourself on that X and look straight ahead at me."

And as soon as I put on my brakes, the camera started clicking. He instructed me to look in every direction ("over your shoulder," "down to the floor," and "directly at the camera like there's a person there") and had me move backward and forward (headshots and full-body shots). It was fun, and I was cooperative.

"You're great in front of the camera," Patrick said.

"Thank you," I said, kind of surprised but also kind of not. I don't get nervous about things and I wasn't nervous about this—I think that helped. Another reason is that I'm confident, whether that's because of the secret modeling program or just a trait of mine, I don't know. It took a couple years after my accident to get to the point of "confidence" in my paralyzed body but, once I accepted and learn to love myself, life is loads easier. For the most part, I'm able to brush off people's rude comments, wear what I want to wear, and interact within my large comfort zone.

Wherever it came from, that confidence made me "great in front of a camera," so the years of acceptance and the middle school secrecy were worth it.

"You know," Patrick said. He was looking at my pictures on the camera's display. "There's a need for people in wheelchairs in advertising. You should send your pictures to agencies and see what happens." He looked up and saw what I guess was my surprise. "I can send you these headshots."

"You think?" I challenged. It seems too good to be true to get paid for my face, even more to get paid to be made up for the camera. "That would be fun. Yes, please send them."

"There's lunch in the cafeteria when you guys are done," another model, male this time, stuck his head through the door and announced. I hadn't thought about food since a very early morning breakfast, but I guess I was a little bit hungry.

"We're done in here," Patrick said. Maybe he could see the excitement on my face this time, too. My face can't hide emotions, apparently. "You can go eat with everyone."

"Great," I said with a smile and turned my wheelchair part way toward the door. "Thank you. Let me know if you need anything else." Like having my face painted, it was fun and I hoped he would call me back but, also, lunch.

————

I arrived in the cafeteria to an impressive sight: silver trays of hot food lined up on a center island and a refrigerator stocked with drinks. I rolled toward the food and one of the models from the hair room.

"Come sit with us when you get your food," she said and moved a chair aside for me.

"I will," I said, impressed with myself for being courted by such a beautiful person. "Thanks."

The silver trays surprised me. Contrary to the assumedly healthy diet a model should follow, they were full of different kinds of noodles, bread, and heavy white sauce. There were also small slices of meat, thank God, so I put one piece of turkey and two carrots on my plate. There was a bucket of sodas and bottles of juice to choose from, but I still chose bottled water.

If I was going to act like a model, I was going to eat like a [stereotypical but apparently not actual] model.

The place at the table with my reserved lack-of-seat was alongside two other models who looked like models, if you know what I mean. I pulled up and, for the most part, they talked and I listened. That's not because I'm shy or antisocial in any way, but they were using modeling industry jargon and I didn't have anything to contribute except for some words I picked up that day: contour, tear sheet, catcall.

This was a new world and I was soaking up all the information. If Patrick follows through and sends me the pictures (he didn't), modeling might be a part of my life. And that would be crazy—the good kind of crazy.

Attention back on lunch: I was the only one eating like a bird, so I daresay the "models don't eat food to stay skinny" stereotype is off. Actually, I was the only one not eating noodles and white sauce.

"When you're done with lunch, don't go home until you check-in with us," announced a woman who looked like she was in charge. "We might need to get more picture or video."

The seasoned models continued to eat their food like they didn't hear anything. Me, Ms. Fish Out of the Tank, made eye contact with the woman and nodded my head in understanding. I was eager, maybe too eager.

I ate my carrots and meat slowly to keep pace with the pasta eaters. Also, I didn't want to draw attention to what I was (or wasn't) eating. Eating in front of people is a fairly constant stress in my life because people just love to comment. I'm often "not eating enough" or "not eating the right things," so I try to fly under the radar as much as possible. People love to comment, and I get tired of hearing it.

The girls at my table slurped their last slurp of white sauce, stuffed the last piece of gluten in their mouths, and we all walked together to the green room to check-in before leaving. I was fitting in well.

"Brittany and Lauren—I need you to stay back," Patrick announced when the pack of us walked through the door. They both nodded their heads and stepped to the side. Suckers. I had fun filming and photographing, but being able to leave was an unexpected relief.

There was one guy behind Patrick, I heard someone call him Greg, saying lines for the video recording. He was beautiful and comfortable in front of the camera so I assumed he was a career model, like most of the girls. Or he completed a secret modeling program when he was young, too.

"Thank you."

"Thank you."

"Thank you."

Everyone except Brittany and Lauren said their thanks and filed out of the room like robots. I was new to this, remember, so I wanted to be more than casual. Also, I wanted to stand out to Patrick so he'd remember to send me those headshots, so I put a little more effort into my departure.

"Thank you for everything."

I followed the flow of girls through the hallway back to our changing room. We all gathered our things: a wardrobe bag that we all had, extra shoes that I didn't think to bring, and personal makeup bags that I definitely did not bring. If I had brought my own makeup, it would have been a Ziploc bag with one mascara wand and a years-old eyeliner tube. Somehow, I seem to have skipped the stage in life where girls learn to apply and wear makeup. If that's a good thing or not, it depends on whom you ask. And I'm not asking anyone.

"See you later," I said to a girl who was standing in front of the door. This was a sweet way of saying "I'm trying to leave, so get out of the way." All of those girls were very friendly, but we were all tired and will probably not see each other again, so not a ton of effort was made.

"It was nice to meet you," she said and moved her tiny feet through the door frame. I had my wardrobe bag on my lap and was on my way out: toward the lobby and to my smiling mom, who had been sitting in the waiting room for me to finish.

"Are you all done?" Mom stood up from an uncomfortable-looking chair when I came into sight.

"Yes," I said. "They said we can leave now."

We scooted through the lobby doors and loaded into the car that was parked in the garage next door.

"He said there's a market for models in wheelchairs," I said once we were settled in the car and driving toward the traffic-packed interstate. "Patrick was the director of the shoot and he said he'd send me my headshots. Maybe this can be a thing I do."

That idea excited me but, I admit, those insecurities from when I was a kid aren't 100% gone. Especially after my disability, I've spent a lot of effort accepting my flaws and differences, so I have more of a "whatever" mentality now. I'm only dealing with a little bit of Kid Kristin's hesitation, but it's still something.

Flash forward a couple weeks and to the apparent end of my modeling career:

No need for any of that "getting over insecurity" business because Patrick forgot about me; my additional words of gratitude were for naught. For that one day, at least, I was a model amongst models. I don't have anything to show for it except an iPhone camera picture that the male model took of me from behind the scenes, but that's enough, I guess.

I was given this opportunity and I took it, to see if I could. Every day there are five, ten devils on my shoulders telling me "your body isn't attractive anymore" and "you're not as good as people who stand up." I'm usually able to swat them down and replace them with angels who say, "you're unique and therefore valuable," but I'm always up for an opportunity to be reassured in disproving the devils.

I was paid for this job so, let's be real, that's also a big factor in my cooperation. That self-esteem boost, though, was at the front. I wanted to prove to myself that, despite my skinnier legs and short stature, my body is still attractive and I'm just as good as people who stand up. I'm still beautiful, regardless of my special condition, but everyone can use a reminder sometimes.

Rowing

"**K**ristin," my coach, Paul, jogged up and said in the same minute of me rolling onto the wooden boards of the dock of Rocketts Landing, an area off the north bank of the James River in Richmond, Virginia. "Go join the others and we'll get you in a boat." I looked beyond his shoulder to a group of about 15 people huddled near the water. "Lisa is going to ride with you today since this is your first time on the water."

The lady standing to the left of Paul was smiling wide. That was probably Lisa.

"Nice to meet you," I said with a smile and an outstretched hand. She didn't offer her hand back to me, likely because she didn't hear me from her position over the ground to gather a pile of straps and buoys. No strike against her.

"We're going to have fun today," she gathered the last strap in her hand, stood up straight, and said. Her smile looked like she really believed it, too. That was refreshing. "Hopefully this storm will hold off."

I nodded my head solemnly and looked up into the drizzling rain. The skies were gray and only just recovered after a day of heavy rain and thunder. A small, secret part of me hoped for rowing practice to get canceled because of it but, with the season end regatta fast approaching, we needed all the practice we could get. There would have to be lightening touching down for Paul to call a cancel.

Lisa was smiling at me in a way that suggested she didn't feel the drizzle or see the gloomy sky at all. If she could still be enthusiastic about riding in the back of a rowboat with a first-time rower and a steady water drip on her head, there certainly wasn't any room for my ill wishes. The wind was blowing in every direction, the air smelled like the impending storm, and there was a dark cloud hanging over the water, threatening to explode at any moment. It was a warm wind and a fresh smell so, if the drizzling rain continued at that muted pace, the conditions for rowing were nearly ideal.

Talk about an attitude shift, huh.

"Okay," Paul said as he walked back up to us. I hadn't even noticed he walked away. "I'll grab your upper body and Lisa will lift your legs to lower you into the seat of the scull."

A "scull" is the name of the thin, borderline-unstable boats used to row. They look almost identical to a kayak, except a scull is skinnier and more precarious. They're also made to sit lower in the water, which translates to the driver of the scull sitting inches away from wet.

He turned his head pointedly toward a squishy cushion on top of a seat that sat upright on the scull's frame. The chair's shoulder-high backrest is a sure sign of its "adaptive" status. The seats are also fixed and stable, as opposed to their normal condition of sitting on a track for the rower to push backward and forward as they row. The configuration of my scull, since I can't use my legs, means I use all arms, all the time.

Paul's hands snaked under my armpits, Lisa grabbed under my knees, they lifted, and they lowered my lanky body onto the seat. Without words, I fastened a strap around my hips and chest. If nothing else, I knew the mechanics of rowing; the Erg machines we'd practiced on for months while waiting on the weather to cooperate enough to get in the water were similar in setup. I looped all the straps, fastened all the Velcro, and grabbed the paddles lying beside me.

Now, I wait for the rest of the team to be ready for launch. That looks like: me, sitting motionless in the front seat of the scull, staring ahead. It feels similar to how a horse must feel as he waits for the gunshot to start a race, ready to explode forward when the gun is fired. Except, imagine: the horse has a broken leg so he missed out on the "explosion" part of the equation. In other words, the myriad of my anticipation to row doesn't necessarily translate to my skill or speed of row.

Regardless, I was eager to get going.

Erg practices every Monday night at the Virginia Boat Club for the past two months prepared me for rowing on the water, at least partially. The Virginia Boat Club is a fancy title for a dark room underneath an even fancier restaurant in Downtown Richmond. Truthfully, I would believe if someone told me there was a murder in that room; the walls were lined with sculls and the lights seemed to always be off. Or maybe there were no lights—I'm not really sure.

Every week, a group of 10-15 wheelchair-bound rowers gathered in the dark and we pushed ourselves for two hours: moving our upper bodies back and forth as hard as we could on stationary Erg seats. That room was either the optimal backdrop for the practice of a team of dedicated rowers, or the perfect setup to a horror movie involving a murder.

I digress.

Now that the weather was warmed, it was time for our much-anticipated row on the James River. All those weeks of Murder Room Erg Training were finally being actualized.

"Whenever you're ready," Lisa yelled from where she sat behind me in the scull. I hadn't noticed her getting in the boat, either. Those people are sneaky. "Lower your paddles in the water and start rowing."

Oh boy, was I ready. I had very little clue what I was doing, but I was ready to do something. I plopped the paddles in the water and pushed off the dock so our scull was pointing toward the middle of the river. Moving purely from my assumptions, I sloshed my paddles in the water and started swishing both then and my body back and forth in a disorganized sequence. I definitely did not know what I was doing.

Lisa let me problem solve those initial movements by myself, which I was grateful. It took a couple of minutes, but I eventually fell into enough of a routine that made me look a little less like a dehydrated fish, and at least halfway composed. All I really did was slow down my arm movements, and I managed to make our scull glide away from the dock and to the middle of the river. Slowly, but we were moving.

"Imagine you're drawing rectangles with your paddles," she yelled up to me.

"Okay," I yelled back, grateful for any advice. I imagine my disorientation looked pretty ridiculous and it might have even been embarrassing if, say, I cared, but I stopped that nonsense long ago. I learned at the beginning of my disability that if I laugh off my shortcomings, people will either empathize with me or laugh alongside me. I can't lose.

I drew rectangles and we picked up a little speed. Lisa mostly stayed quiet, with the exception of a rare tip like "sink your right paddle deeper in the water" and "don't bring your left hand so close to your body." Other than those things, though, I was feeling pretty good about myself. We were moving over the water consistently and both of our bodies were still dry, so there's not a ton more she could have asked for. I'll count that as a win.

"You're a natural," Lisa yelled up to me. I felt like I was definitely doing some things incorrectly, so it was exciting for her to say that. The Virginia humidity had blown up and unstraightened my hair, so I just felt a little off. "I think we'll put you on a solo boat next week."

"Cool," I yelled back. I hadn't fallen in love with rowing yet, but independence is always my goal. Cutting the tape on a solo boat this early in the game, though, is a fast track I felt ready for.

That being said, I also acknowledge that I have no idea how to steer the boat; Lisa was 100% taking care of that part. I'll cross that bridge when I get to it, I guess. In the ambiguous world of disability, the only perspective that works is: go with the flow.

————

When a friend suggested I try adaptive rowing, I remembered how much I disliked the sport when I tried it many years ago. This experience made me realize that all I've tried is adaptive kayaking. The difference? It's like black and white, and I like rowing tons more. The oar used for kayaking isn't secured to anything so, in my experience, trying to control it is like trying to control a wild bird using only my hands. That is, impossible. Unless I can find something stable to push off from with my oar, my boat pretty much sits still.

A scull, if you haven't already inferred, is set up with what looks like two half-length oars secured to the boat on either side of me. The benefit of a secured oar is it eliminates the possibility of me losing my grip, the oar sinks in the water, and I'm left to pray myself back to the shore. Because of the oar's fastening to the boat, I don't have to depend solely on my abdomen muscles, which are not the most reliable, to keep me sitting straight up; fixed oars allow me to transfer some weight and lean into my strokes. This is significant especially for me, Ms. Lack of Usable Back Muscle. A chest strap, which doubles as a very dramatic pushup bra, also helps keep me upright.

On the other end, attached oars mean I can't dig them into the ground and push off like I did in my kayaking lesson. In harsher words, I can't cheat. I suppose this is good because it forces me to work harder, but it's bad because I don't have a free hand to scratch my nose or swipe the hair out of my eye when the wind blows just right. This is a surprisingly significant setback of rowing in a scull. To reiterate, it's just harder work.

"We should go back to the dock and switch out," Lisa yelled again. "I think there are a couple of people waiting to get in."

Remember: light rain. The overcast sky made for a beautiful and enjoyable day on the water, but also a humorously unattractive time for my hair, which I forgot to tie back. I was willing to go back to the dock, if only for that reason. That sounds silly and vain of me, but loose hair is annoying and it's not a good feeling to feel unattractive. I know you know this, ladies.

"Good plan," I said. I drew my rectangles and sunk my right paddle deep in the water until Lisa took over and parked us parallel to the dock's ledge.

Paul was waiting on the dock beside my parked wheelchair with outstretched arms, I guess in anticipation for an armpit dig-and-lift. Lisa was the first to climb out of the scull, snatch under my knees, and the two of them airlifted me to my wheelchair cushion in one smooth and quick motion. I could tell they had done it 1,000 times before by their lack of communication and seemingly minimal thought that went into the transfer. Thank God for helpers like that.

"She was great," Lisa bragged to Paul.

The word "great" felt like an exaggeration but, if she was dropping those kinds of adjectives, it felt good to be on the receiving end. They looked at me with big, inspired eyes. The rain was starting to fall harder so I didn't have a clear image of their faces, but I imagine that's what they were: big and inspired. I'll add the words "impressed" and "in awe" while we're at it.

"That was fun," I said to the pair of them. I was a little bit out of breath from my hustle back to the dock, but I still wasn't as worn out as I had hoped. "Thank you, guys, for helping."

I waved my hand as a gesture of "goodbye" and turned to leave. I didn't linger on the dock for too long because they had other rowers to airlift, plus the rain was making me look goofier by the minute. There was an attractive rower, the same guy from tennis practice, on the other side of the dock and I didn't want him to see me so off my game.

Being a girl is too stressful sometimes.

"See you next week, Kristin," Paul said to the back of my head. I turned to nod an acknowledgement, and saw Lisa beaming a smile beside him.

The rain started coming down harder, so I left the group on the dock to soak. It wasn't falling hard enough to cancel practice for the other rowers, but it was enough for me to be thankful to be leaving.

My afro and I said a final "goodbye" to the crew of rowers and friends huddled on the dock. I, we, turned my wheelchair toward the land and, quite literally, I slid down the wet sidewalk to my car.

Rappelling

I've never been so high in my life. Everything I saw was beautiful and, an almost uncomfortable amount, I wasn't in charge of anything that was happening to me. It was almost as if I was watching myself from a bird's eye.

To clarify: this isn't a story about me doing drugs—this is about rappelling off the side of a twenty-story-high building in Virginia Beach, Virginia.

─────

Five months prior to my jump, my friend told me about a rappelling event purposed to raise money and awareness for a residential community for adults with special needs. True to my reputation, I jumped on the opportunity and began the application process; there was a solid 15 seconds between my hearing about the event, contemplating risk, and reserving my spot. In case it isn't clear and with evidence from my eBay purchase history, my reputation is: impulse.

In the five months between registering and rappelling, please believe I forgot almost completely about it. That meant I missed my opportunity to be nervous or overthink anything; I registered for it with my figurative eyes closed, and now it was time to jump off a building with my figurative and, at times, literal eyes closed. When the day of the event finally came, I brought the Beale and Gilman families, consisting of my parents, sister Jessica, and her husband Tyler, along with me.

———

"Do you know where to go?" Dad asked in a hurried voice. We were late for the Pre-Jump Training because we had some navigation problems getting there. Admitting my faults here: I was in charge of the GPS and led us in the opposite direction and into a thirty-minute detour. In my defense, I have my father's sense of direction.

"Second floor," I responded with halfway fake happiness and halfway genuine excitement. My directional mistake was a little bit of a wet blanket, and everyone was stressed. This wasn't the first time I've made the Entering The Wrong City Into GPS mistake, so I'm arguing that it's also kind of their fault for putting me in charge. Right?

———

The five of us loaded into the hotel's elevator and got off at the second ding. A table was set up immediately in front of us and, behind it, a plump woman with round eyes was sitting there, smiling. She was guarding the entrance to a large room that I could see only a sliver of. On the table in front of her there was a clipboard with a long list of names.

"Are you Kristin Beale?" she asked with a timbre of excitement. There's no such thing as mystery when you're in a wheelchair.

"Yes," I said with matched enthusiasm. I was only at the check-in table and the wet blanket was starting to dry.

"Kristin," another man lunged into the scene and near-shouted. I'm not sure where he came from, but I was thankful for his enthusiasm. "I'm Greg. We talked on the phone."

I have no memory of talking to Greg on the phone, but I played it off well.

"Yes," I said with fake recollection and, still, genuine excitement. "It's good to put a face to a voice."

"Let's get you over here and strapped up." He pointed to another man in the large room who waved his hands spastically at me. The man was close to my age and was holding a handful of harness.

"Nice to meet you," the new guy said. "Greg told me all about you. My name is Peter."

If Greg had the ability to tell Peter "all about me," I must have talked to him on the phone, after all. Okay, fine.

Peter smiled another wide one and got to work immediately. He pointed to my leg as if to say, "can I have that?" I shook my head for yes, he plucked it from my footplate, and started pulling carabiners out of his pockets like he was a magician and they were bunnies.

I pushed up on my tires to lift my body, and Peter buckled and yanked what seemed like 100 fastenings. His hands swarmed around me until I was fully outfitted in a harness system that pulled over my shoulders, wrapped around my torso, and tangled around my thighs. It was very snug, and the finished product was not unlike a pushup bra. There were no attractive men around me, though, so that was a waste.

"Have you been doing this long?" I asked Peter. I was curious for the answer but, more, I just wanted conversation. Even now that I was at the event, I still wasn't feeling scared about the jumping-off-a-building part of this at all; the full danger of the sport hadn't even crossed my mind. I'm not sure if that comes from confidence in the carabiners, or my reckless imperilment, but my lack of reflection sure makes things go smoother.

"I'm one of the only full-time employees and I've been with this company for three years," he said. His voice was distracted because he was attaching and locking something like eight carabiners to the loops and holes on my outfit.

"Seems like a really fun job," I said with much, maybe too much, enthusiasm.

"I'll explain what these are for as soon as I get them all on," he said in that same distracted voice. Small Talk Time was over.

His hands crawled around me, he tightened all carabiners one more time, then gave everything a final tug. No surprise, he pulled more bunnies (carabiners) out of his pocket and screwed them to a hook coming out of my pushup bra harness.

"I'll help with the seat," Greg came back from somewhere behind us and said. He held up a rectangle cut of thick, five-inch-wide fabric. "This goes under your butt. Since you can't push off with your legs, you're going to sit on this while you go down."

He slapped the middle of the rectangle and I took that as instruction to push up on the tires of my wheelchair so my hips would levitate above the seat, and they could slide it under. I pushed my body up and the two men wedged and positioned it under my butt, right in the spot for me to fall in the center when I lowered back down. Greg laid a pair of leather gloves and a blue helmet in my lap, nodded his head hard one time, and the two of us turned toward the elevator leading to the roof.

"Bye, guys" I turned to my family and said with a big ol' smile. Dad, whom I was seeing for the first time since we arrived at training, was standing next to them in a helmet and harness outfit of his own.

"I'm going up there with you," he said. "I'll move your wheelchair to the ground so it'll be there when you get to the bottom."

"Great," I said with a smile and relief that I didn't expect. It was cool that he got to go to the roof with me. I like when Dad is around.

————

When the three of us reached the top floor, the roof, I rolled out and was hit by the beauty of the ocean in front of us: the water was three different shades of blue; a warm, Spring wind was blowing; and little ant people were playing on the sand below. I could have easily spent the afternoon up there.

But, actually, I was on that roof to do the exact opposite.

"Kristin," a new voice shouted to me. I turned from looking at the water and saw a man bouncing toward me. "It's great to have you. Are you excited?" I smiled big and it felt excessive. My smile was in lieu of words, though, so it worked. "I'll show you how we're doing this. Come over here."

The roof wasn't very big, so I rolled only five feet before I reached him. Dad was trailing me close.

"I'm Mike," he said with a small wave. "I'll explain our setup."

He first held up a descender, or belay device, that looks very similar to an emergency brake in a car.

"Use this handle to control the speed of your fall," he said. "You can pause your rappel by lifting the handle. If you start falling too fast, pull it harder for a safety stop."

But I wasn't planning on going fast—I wanted to take it in.

"Okay," I said and nodded. "Got it."

"Good. We'll be watching you at the top to make sure nothing goes wrong," he assured. "Now, are you ready to go?"

"I'm ready," I half-shouted, louder than I expected. I was using my Outside Voice but, also, I was eager.

Mike started pulling bunnies from his jacket just like Peter did, only this time to connect me to a stationary crane-looking device against the roof's edge.

"I'm going to lift you up now, okay?" Mike asked. It was more of a narration and less than a question, so I just smiled. I didn't know what he meant by "lift you up," so I was just going with it.

He nodded once and started cranking, tightening, and yanking on the rope until I was levitating one foot above my wheelchair cushion. This part was fun. If my rappel turned out to be weird and terrifying, that rooftop levitation would maybe make all the trouble worthwhile. Maybe?

He stopped cranking the machine when I was floating fully midair with the open sea in front of me and ant people hundreds of feet below me. Two other men stepped up to connect and tighten my carabiners to another tower of straps sitting nearby until my harness was connected to pulleys and fastenings from my all sides. All I could do was dangle there and smile, allowing my body to be positioned and pulled in every direction. It was great.

"You're crazy, girl," I heard Dad shout before the ropes started moving me over the edge into starting position. He was standing in front of me on the roof, but I wished he was getting ready to rappel beside me.

"All right," said a new, unidentified man. Where were all these people coming from? "Here we go."

Even from the perspective of hanging twenty stories above a deadly concrete sidewalk, I managed to still be excited and feel pretty good about what I was doing. Chalk that up to being a thrill-seeker, I guess.

I winked at Dad, which means a hard blink, released the emergency brake, and started to drop.

"Go slow, Kristin," I told myself out loud. The wind was blowing hard and I was far enough from the roof for no one to hear me talking to myself and call me a loony. "Take it in."

————

I tried to go slow—I really did. Believe me: I definitely had the urge to zip down the edge of the building at top speed, but I fought it. My years of skiing straight down a snow slope without using breaks or turns is either evidence that I love to faceplant, or I have a little bit of a "need for speed," excuse my cliché. I wanted to let myself fall free down the building, but I fought it. After all, I may not get this opportunity until the event next year, and that's only wishful thinking.

On the way down, I tried to turn my head toward the ocean as much as possible so I could enjoy the enormous view, but it was tricky. Imagine a hairdryer when the cord is twisted tight. To untangle it, suspend the dryer in the air so it'll spin around very fast for the cord to return to baseline. In this example, my body is the twirling hard dryer and the carabiner straps are the electrical cord. As much as I wanted to turn and see the horizon, all I could do was spin in place.

In the seconds I was able to face the horizon, though, it was huge and beautiful. Virginia Beach is unique in that there isn't much to the waves when you're a kid and want to play in them, but the lack of tall waves is the reason it's beautiful to look at when you're a more boring adult and don't want to get in. From the perspective of me, dangling way above sea-level, "beautiful" doesn't do it justice.

———

"KRISTIN," I heard the crowd beneath me screaming as I got closer to the ground. They were saying things like "YOU GO, GIRL," and "YOU'RE DOING GREAT." I looked down and saw my ant mom holding my ant dog. Ant Dad, Ant Jessica, and Ant Tyler were down there somewhere, but I couldn't pick them out. There was a larger group of ants standing in a huddle and screaming up to me, and that was exciting. I don't know where all the ants came from, but they knew my name enough to cheer for me. I have no complaints.

———

When I got to the bottom of the building, I slowed my descent and spun in circles until I should have felt nauseous. I spun into arm's reach distance from the ground, and two men grabbed my legs to guide my levitating body to my wheelchair that Dad transported from the rooftop and positioned in the middle of a flowerbed for my return.

In the seconds after my butt hit my seat's cushion, my dog, Achilles, jumped from Mom's arms and into my lap. She was going bananas, like I was returning from a three-month-long vacation. As if I would ever go on vacation without her. Thank God for dogs and their lack of perception of time.

"That was awesome," Jessica said, following closely behind Achilles. Her enthusiasm was only slightly less. Mom, Dad, and Tyler were following close behind her, all smiling big. "You did great. Very cool."

"Did you see me?" I asked eagerly. It was a silly question because she had literally just acknowledged my fall, but I wanted to talk about it more. "It was so cool." Jessica nodded hard and slapped me on the back—in a good way.

The huddle of ants I saw from the sky started to migrate to where we were standing. I later found out they all worked with Dad, but for now they were just enthusiastic strangers.

"That was awesome," a woman shouted to me.

"Great job" another, slightly more recognizable woman said. I recognized their congratulations as similar to what I hear when I finish a marathon, but this was far less work than handcycling 26.2 miles.

"You were flying down that building," another one, a man this time, said.

"Was I?" I asked, surprised. "I tried to go slowly."

"Yeah," he continued. "You were much faster than everyone else."

Everyone else must have inch-wormed down. That's not my problem.

"That was awesome, sweetie," Dad said, put his hand on my shoulder, and looked down at me. I think I saw his eyes fill with water, but I could be making that up.

"Thanks," I exulted. Everything was happy and my body was buzzing. Also, my front wheelchair wheels were sinking deeper into the soil we were standing in—I could feel it happening. "Let's go back to the room," I said and popped a wheelie to roll out of the soil.

I said "goodbye" and "thank you for coming" to the crowd of strangers in the most honest way I could manage, then let the back of Jessica's head lead me onto the sidewalk. She was moving toward the double doors of the same building I had just fallen from, into the elevator, and back to the conference room.

"Did you have fun?" Greg asked when the five of us entered. "I heard you did a great job."

Word travels fast, I guess.

"I had tons of fun," I said. "That was good."

"I'm glad," he said with a smile that seemed genuine. "I'm glad you got to do this." We smiled at each other for one more long second.

"Is this your only bag?" Jessica asked from behind us. She was gathering belongings quickly so we could get out of there and start back home.

"That's all," I said. I turned my body away from Greg and saw that people were rushing around, pulling out bunnies, and training more rappelers.

"Thank you, everyone," I shouted as a blanket of gratitude to the helpers in the room. Most didn't hear me because they were otherwise distracted, but I did hear a "you're welcome" and "you're very pretty."

I may have misunderstood that last one, but I wasn't going to push it.

Jessica grabbed my single bag and I said another "goodbye" and "see you next year" to Greg. Again, wishful thinking.

"The elevator is over here," Jessica directed.

I followed her to the opposite wall, and she gushed about the event and my rappelling the whole elevator ride to meet the rest of the family in the building's lobby. I took it in, soaked it up.

In my post-injured life, I don't take for granted when people are impressed with or compliment something I've done. It's so much better than pity, the alternative. In this case, I was able to rappel alongside able bodies without my sport being put into an "adaptive" category. In my opinion, adaptive sports and the overall lifestyle of a wheelchair user is more fun, but sometimes assimilation can be a relief. It's rare, but sometimes.

"I'm tired," Jessica looked at me and said.

This was funny because she was tired from spectating, and I was still running on adrenaline. Does anyone have a handcycle? I'll bike back to Richmond.

Just kidding. I guess I was a tiny bit tired, too.

"So am I," I said and smiled up at her.

"I'm proud of you, Keeks," she said as the elevator dinged and we stepped out to meet Mom and Dad in the lobby. "Today was fun."

Golfing

"I'm here for a golf lesson," I told a middle-aged man standing behind the counter in a small, stinky pro shop. "My name is Kristin Beale."

"Kristin," he said with a wide smile. "I'm expecting you. Wait while I get you a club." He turned on his heel, disappeared through a door behind the counter, and left me waiting for his return. I noticed another man standing in the corner behind me, but he was silent in my background; I was distracted by the one getting my equipment and was unsure if this one wanted to talk, so I left the Conversation Ball in his court.

"What other sports do you play?" the man in the corner spoke up after minutes passed of us mutually ignoring each other.

"I'm on tennis and rowing teams, but the seasons ended last week," I said, aware of how much of a loony I was about to seem. I paused for a moment to read his face. He seemed interested, so I continued. "I'm learning to play lacrosse next week, and I'm rappelling off a building in a couple months. I've tried skiing, surfing, and archery, but I don't do those anymore. I've completed eight marathons on a handcycle, which is my favorite sport. My first marathon was 2011."

The man was watching me with his eyebrows raised into his low hairline. Part of me hoped he would suggest another sport to try, and part of me just wanted the conversation to be over. I didn't want to talk about myself anymore.

"You're quite an athlete," the middle-aged man said and reappeared from behind the door. I turned back to him and smiled my appreciation. "My name is Tim and I'll be teaching your lesson today." He continued. "Tennis and lacrosse will both help you with golfing."

"Great," I said with a smile and nod. That sounded correct in theory, but I had a pretty solid hunch that my golf game would be lamentable, regardless of my athleticism.

"What made you interested in golfing?" Tim asked.

"I played a couple of times when I was a kid and didn't like it," I replied. Not the best way to win him over. "Adaptive sports are so different from regular sports, though, so I'm giving it a second chance in my wheelchair." His face was frozen in a smile that I couldn't tell was fake or not, so I kept talking. "I grew up in a golf neighborhood and my parents love to play, so I thought I might like it." I stopped for a couple of seconds to smile back at him. "Also, the Paragolfer looks like fun. I kind of just want to try it."

My attitude toward second chances doesn't apply only to sports; whether it's because of my maturity or my changed perspective thanks to my disability, I've found love and preference in a number of unexpected and previously-written-off places. There's nothing like acquiring a disability to make me reassess opportunities and people in my life.

That perspective is what I have to thank for my ending up in this stinky pro shop on a stiflingly hot afternoon of summer.

"Let's get you set up, then." he said and relaxed the probably-fake smile. He turned around and pointed his tiny hand toward the door on the opposite wall. I took his direction, rolled through the glass threshold, and onto the humongous green lawn. I felt a bead of sweat gather underneath my sports bra and I fought back the instinct to turn around, roll back to the air conditioning, and yell "Nope" as a point to everyone in the clubhouse that I am a lady and ladies should not be outside in this heat.

Instead, true to my "Try Everything Twice" intention, I rolled right into it and realized it was also very humid. Wonderful.

"I learned to use the Paragolfer three years ago when I started working here," Tim said as we walked and rolled onto the grass. "We've been trying to get more people in wheelchairs to come out and use this thing, but you're only our second." He turned his head and gave me a meaningful look. "We don't get to use it often. We're glad to have you."

I smiled back at him and we shared a hot second, literally, of connection.

"Let's get started over here," he said, walking in front of me. Again, he raised that tiny hand and pointed at what I assumed was the Paragolfer parked at the edge of the lawn. It just looked like a motorized wheelchair, except bigger. There were two monster-sized wheels that sat under a solid metal, white frame. On top of the frame, there was a black seat with a high backrest and a Velcro strap that fell lazily onto the seat's cushion. Attached to the bottom of the frame near the wheels, there was a thick, metal footplate to match the industrial-sized theme of the machine. The only exciting thing about the chair, that I could tell, was the small remote control perched at an arm's distance from the backrest.

A remote control, in this context, can only mean one thing: motorized.

"Go ahead and transfer into the seat and we'll get you strapped in," Tim ordered. "Have you ever used one of these before?"

"No," I said. "I'm excited to see how it works."

Translation: I'm excited to get in the chair so I can push buttons and zoom around the lawn. A motorized wheelchair is something I've never wished to need to use, but it is fun to try—if only for 30 minutes.

Once I transferred into the chair, Tim swarmed around me like a mosquito: connecting straps, pulling strings, and tightening a wide harness that reached from my belly button to my chest. The harness, along with being the most conspicuous ingredient of the setup, is the most important part because it functions to keep me from eating dirt when I lean to hit the golf ball. Also, it helps my confidence in standing up; minimal back and abdomen muscles make any kind of upright movement difficult because of swaying hips and a collapsing torso, so a tight corset is ideal.

Finally, Tim pushed the power button and took two steps away from me. Without speaking, he admired his handiwork with a cheesy smile on his face. I took that cheese smile as a sign of his being done with my setup, and snatched the remote control from its perch next to my leg. I mashed my finger on a button advertising a small, green arrow, and jolted forward.

It felt like the "fun joke" people sometimes play in the car by tapping on the brakes to give their passengers several tiny whiplashes from the car's jolts. My friends used to do that when we were in high school because I guess they thought it was funny, but it's not funny. It hurts.

"Motor yourself over to the red line," Tim said and pointedly looked behind me. I wondered if he had seen my initial, spastic movements with the Paragolfer. He wasn't smirking and seemed to still have a level of respect toward me, so I assume he hadn't. "Let's get you up and start golfing."

With caution and less enthusiasm this time, I lightly pressed the green arrow and eased into movement. The chair glided over the grass to the red line painted on the ground, where I lightly pressed the red circle on the remote to stop. I'm wise to that machine now.

"Okay," he instructed and pointed his finger at my remote. "You can push this button to make yourself stand up." I followed his finger to a button on the remote that said *Up*. "Go slowly so you don't get lightheaded."

I followed directions in pushing the button, but I didn't go slowly; I was too excited to stand upright to go slow. I don't get lightheaded when I stand anymore either, thank God. In most cases, lightheadedness is a significant problem for people in wheelchairs due to our compromised blood flow that comes from sitting down all the time. I had serious lightheadedness problems in the initial months after my accident that rendered me unable to even sit up in bed without one or two stops along the way. Because wheelchair users are sedentary, it takes a conscious effort to keep moving around. Combating a light head, among other things, is a reward for that conscious effort. Thank God, I'll say it again, lightheadedness doesn't hold me back anymore.

When my body was fully upright and I was confident my hips and lower body weren't going to slide out of the straps and to the ground, I looked around at the beautiful day. I say the word "beautiful" based off how it looked, not how it felt. The combination of Virginia humidity and a 92-degree forecast made it feel like I was in the living room of a burning house. The scenery of the driving range was beautiful with rolling hills that touched the horizon, but even that was difficult to appreciate with how my body felt. The golf range was visually beautiful, physically my nightmare.

Now that I've set the scene, here's the important part: I was upright. The Paragolfer allowed me to stand up tall, and even the heat couldn't ruin that for me.

"Here you go," Tim said. He stepped forward and handed me the rubber handle of a golf club. I had forgotten about his existence with all the excitement of standing up and looking around. "Okay," he continued and bent over to put a golf ball on the grass in front of my toes. "Position the head of your club close behind the ball."

He crammed his hands on the club's shaft above and below mine and guided the club's head toward the ball.

"Got it," I said in attempt to talk him off my club. I recognize he was just trying to help, but his breath was too close to mine. Those tiny hands were annoying me.

"When you feel ready, swing the club high behind you and make your shot," he instructed and stepped off my club.

I felt ready. My club's head was touching the ball, my body was hunched over and not spilling to the ground, and I had the height advantage of an able-bodied golfer. If you could somehow not see the huge machine I was attached to, I would look like a fully capable golf pro.

That was a joke. It's impossible to not see that machine. That's like telling someone to not see my left eyeball when looking at my face.

I readjusted my club to rest on the ball's back and slayed it behind me for a powerful hit. When it came back down, I felt great and had good intentions, but I missed my target by about three inches. I wish the thought really did count.

The power of my failed shot unearthed a fat chunk of grass that went flying ahead of me where the ball should have been. It was as if the grass was mocking me.

I yelled "*whoops*" in a high-pitched voice and laughed in a way that sounded like I was throwing up—as if that would make anything better. I wanted anyone who saw my shot to laugh with me aloud, not at me in their heads.

Turns out, no one cared and seemingly no one even saw my shot. All eyes were not on Kristin, thank God.

"Ready for your next ball?" Tim asked. I snapped back into Business Determined Mode and nodded my head for "yes." He put another ball at my toes and I, again, psyched myself up to take the shot.

After a fail like my first one, I hesitated for a moment before leaning forward for the next hit. I could feel myself getting less and less attractive with every degree of Virginia heat but, out of the corner of my eye, I saw a lady taking a picture of me. It could have also been a picture of something I was standing close to but, just in case, I stood up straight and tried to look my cutest. I didn't know who she was but, if a strange woman is going to have a picture of me on her cell phone, I at least want to look good in it.

"Do you want some water?" Tim asked when he noticed my delay. I pulled my mind back to the golfing situation.

"Yes," I said. My voice came out sounding like a dry, old woman. "Yes please."

Tim speed-walked back to the clubhouse and reappeared seconds later with a paper triangle of water. If I wasn't concerned with looking my best and keeping the equipment dry, I would have dumped that triangle on my head and face.

Alas, I am a lady.

I took a mouthful of water and hung the cup by my side. The water, ironically, tasted like a golf ball. A lukewarm, thermoplastic golf ball.

"Thank you," I said in the sweetest voice I could manage with the heat and growing fatigue of my body.

"You're welcome," he said. "Are you ready to keep going?" I nodded my head and smiled—only kind of fake.

Tim fed me a few more balls that I missed. But I did more than just miss the ball, thank you very much. I missed the balls, but I substituted each of them with chunks of grass. My consistency counts for something, right?

It also may have worked to my advantage: my hope was to trick everyone who was watching me (nobody) into thinking I was actually making the shots. They think they're watching the ball fly through the air, only to squint and see that it's an entire ant community unearthed from the driving range. Aside from the rare person who looks at the world through squinted eyes, I may have tricked a few.

As minutes passed standing in the heat, I cared less and less about my performance. Honestly, I just wanted to go back to the clubhouse, the air conditioning, the haven.

"A couple more shots and you'll be ready to go professional," a new man walked from behind me and exclaimed. Either he hadn't been watching my execution or he was making an ironic jest about my lack thereof, because nothing about me said "professional." Even so, his flattery gave me a streak of energy and I threw my head back with laughter. It wasn't nearly as funny as I reflected, but I was feeding my audience. I managed a hearty fake laugh.

"I like your confidence," I said with a big smile. "Don't watch me anymore because I don't want you to lose it." I was also kidding, but kind of not.

"Hey, Dylan," a woman yelled at the new man from just outside the clubhouse. Dylan turned his body toward her and waved. He stared at her for another moment before turning back to me with a broad smile that showed most of his teeth. It was kind of a weird moment between the three of us, but it served a purpose: I learned the new man's name is Dylan.

"Oh shoot," I said as soon as Dylan turned back to me and finished his smile. "While you weren't looking, I hit a ball straight ahead on the range," I said and pointed my finger 1,000 yards to the end of the course. We both knew this couldn't be true, so I continued. "My form was perfect, and it flew high."

"Did you?" Dylan asked with a big smile and raised eyebrows. "Great job."

I kept his eye contact for another second and he was too genuine; Dylan's smile made me unsure if he truly believed me or was just playing along. I would feel a little guilty if he believed my trick.

"No," I confessed. "It's right there."

I pointed to the ball sitting ten feet away from my toes and watched Dylan's eyebrows return to their spot above his eyes. I almost tricked him into thinking I made the greatest shot but, in reality, I made the lamest shot. Dylan gave me a weak smile, turned around, and walked toward the clubhouse.

―――――

I went through about forty balls that afternoon. I was improving a little bit, though: of the forty, I missed about fifteen; successfully hit eight; and the remaining seventeen were shot to the far left side of the green. I can assure you that all except those eight successful balls were followed by either my accidental snort or a forced and unnecessarily loud laugh. I was trying to play it cool—I really was. I guess my thought was that if I was going to be paired with that bulky, attention-grabbing machine, I should be at least kind of good at golf. Since that skill was unattainable to me, I was creating distractions after every bad shot, making my performance a bit more bearable. Something like that.

Again, to remind you, no one was watching me.

"I would love more water," I said to Tim. It tasted like a golf ball, but even that's better than the dry mouth I was maintaining. Dry mouth combined with humidity-frizzed hair and probably a wet circle of under-boob sweat on my shirt, and I was looking good. Sexy, I daresay.

Just kidding. Totally kidding.

"We're pretty much done for today," Tim said. "You can get back in your wheelchair and get water inside." Praise God. It was too hot to golf, especially since I can hardly hit enough balls to call it "golfing."

I pushed the *Down* button on my remote control and descended back to sitting height. Once the machine bumped to a stop, I immediately pushed the green arrow to glide back to the clubhouse. My immediacy had a lot to do with the heat, but also because I was excited to motor-ride over the bumpy grass of the lawn.

"Good job out there," Dylan reappeared once I was inside and announced. Again, I'm unsure whether he really thought I did a good job or just loved the irony, but I smiled big anyway. It was nice of him to either believe in me or just to acknowledge my golf game, so a smile felt like a good response. "I hope you'll come play with us again."

"I might," I said.

Keyword: might.

My smile was big and my body language was affirming to distract from my floppy response. The possibility of me ever participating in golfing again lies less in my interest in the sport and desire to get better, and more in whether I want another chance to zoom around in the Paragolfer. That actually, might be enough.

The reason I tried golfing in the first place was merely to step out of my comfort zone—outside the comfort of old, familiar activities and the very literal comfort of air conditioning. Even if I never return to the sport, I had the opportunity that afternoon to stand up tall. And that, I reiterate, is worth enduring anything—even adaptive golfing.

Skydiving

This is called "skydiving," but it was really just a levitation. More specifically, I was levitating over a wind tunnel blowing 120mph air at me, up my nose, into my cheeks.

I imagine pictures of my experience would look like the pictures people post that are never ever flattering, but almost a requirement after an airplane jump. For whatever reason, people just love to share those pictures from, hopefully, the least attractive point in their lives: goofy smiles on wind-warped faces taken mid-jump and from the worst possible angle. Usually, the pictures are taken at the moment when the wind blows the person's lips up, creating a Halloween-status tooth and gum combination. Those are either the best or worst pictures, depending on your motives.

For my skydiving experience there were no cameras and no attractive men as far as I could see, so I was free to be as ugly as I needed. I was on a weekend trip to Virginia Beach organized around adaptive surfing but I, having surfed in California waters a couple of years before and didn't feel the need to freeze cold in Virginia waters to try it again, decided to skydive instead. I was in another city, there were no cameras, no attractive men, and I was free.

———

"Do you want to fly today?" a teenage-looking boy came to me and asked.

"I want to," I said.

"Okay. I'll tell you how this works." He straightened his back up to stand tall. "We're going to push your wheelchair to that door," he said and pointed to the skinny entrance. "The two of us are going to lift you into the dome," he said and nodded his head over my shoulder to a stronger-looking man standing near the door. "Then the air will turn on and you'll start to fly."

First of all, there's no need for any of these strangers to push my wheelchair. Second, there had to be something he wasn't mentioning—that sounded too easy.

To set this scene more, I'll explain the unique circumstances of an indoor skydiving facility. Trying to recreate the unpredictable and unstable environment of an airplane jump is, by nature, impossible to do, but they got it pretty close. The facility is a warehouse-like building with a two-story-high glass dome set in the middle of it. At the bottom of the dome, there's a skinny door that leads to a skinny bridge that spans the length of the dome. Looking below the bridge, there are something like ten high powered fans to levitate the flyer and crowd the floor.

Lined around the dome, there are two rows of wooden benches for people to wait for their fly time and/or laugh at the wind-warped faces of fellow levitators. At least, that's what I was doing.

"Got it," I said and gave a polite and only kind of fake smile.

"There are a few more things to go over with you," he continued, still standing tall. "Each flying session lasts two minutes. It's too loud in there for dialogue, so we created our own language." His hand formed a thumbs up. "When you do this, it means 'all good.'" He pointed his finger at the ground. "This means 'don't go so high.'" He changed into a thumbs down. "And this means 'I've had enough.'"

"Okay," I said, the response he wanted to hear. "Great."

"Put this on," he said and handed me a pile of navy fabric, "and I'll get you the rest of your gear." I unfolded a very baggy one-piece jumpsuit that had carabiners, Velcro straps, and linen handles at every fold. I feel confident that costume only goes through the washing machine on an annual basis. It didn't smell badly, but I was catastrophizing a nervous and sweaty teenager wearing the same suit just before I was about to touch it to my exposed skin. So that was good.

"I also have these for you," the teenager said. He held out his hand, presenting me with neon orange earplugs to protect my one remaining healthy eardrum, and clear glasses to protect my pupils from drying out.

"After you put that on," his eyes shot to the jumpsuit," go over there and get a helmet." He pointed to a wall lined with black helmets, ranging from size mouse to monster.

"Thanks," I said and bent over to put the earplugs and glasses on the ground.

To put on the suit, I first lift my left leg to lace it through the hole, put it down and pull, lift my right leg, pull, unweight my left hip, pull, unweight right hip, pull, drape my upper body over my thigh, lift up and pull, sit back up and wiggle around in my seat. For the arms, I lace one after another, pull the fabric to my shoulders, and zip the zipper to my chin.

When I was first injured, the only way I could put on pants was lying in a bed to thrash back and forth and unweight. Understandably, that made going in public and having to use the public restroom very unappealing. At this point, more than 15 years into my disability, I'm able to put on my pants while sitting down. It's an achievement, not necessarily a traditional achievement, but it makes going out in public and to other people's houses a whole lot more attractive.

"I have your helmet over here," I heard a female voice say from behind me. I turned and saw that, actually, she was talking directly to me. "Do you need a small or a medium?"

"Medium," I said with no hesitation. I learned from my trial-and-error trying to find a bike helmet that, despite the rest of my body being a size small, my head needs size medium.

"Okay," she said. "Here you are." She handed me a sleek, black helmet that reminded me of the one my parents made me wear while riding my bike as a kid.

"Thank you," I said and tried it on for size. I put on the clear glasses, leaned over to see in the mirror behind her, and I looked like a bug. A cute, dateable bug, but a bug nonetheless.

"Ma'am," the teenage boy shouted from behind me. "It's your turn to fly." I smiled a goodbye to the helmet lady and rolled to where the boy stood. "Park over here," he pointed to the ground next to him, "and we'll carry you in. Then the air will turn on and you'll fly."

"Got it," I said. The instructions were very basic: park, be carried, fly. I can do that.

In one motion, the stronger man lifted me from my wheel-chair seat and squeezed us through the door. Like the teenager said, the dome was too loud for conversation between us, so the only thing we exchanged was a head nod and thumbs up.

Almost instantly after entering, the air turned on and we began to rise. He must have been holding on to one of my linen handles, because he stayed by my side the whole way up—about 100 feet. My upper body was in control, grabbing onto his elbows, but my paralyzed legs had a mind of their own; they were flying in every direction, nearly to embarrassment.

I say "nearly" because, again, no cameras and no attractive men. I was free.

We, my maniacal legs, my reasonably attractive flying partner and I, were flying in the air and I felt great. Before my turn and from my place at the wooden benches, I watched the flips, dips, and turns of my peers, and concluded that I would likely be the first of the day to blow chunks in the wind stream. I decided to fly, anyway, because throwing up in a wind chamber would be a great story to tell, right? A great story, only after two to three days to recover from my embarrassment.

Alas, I didn't get sick and I continue to be a lady. We dipped, bobbed, and spun around for the whole two minutes. Two minutes goes by quickly in the dome, but I'm not confident my tummy would be able to handle much longer.

A giant timer outside the dome's wall indicated the final 10 seconds of my fly time. I made eye contact with my instructor for what I think was the first time, and realized we forgot to talk about how I was getting out of there. He looked at me with a look that intended "this is the end—stop smiling," and I snapped back to Logistical Planning Mode for my return to my wheelchair. The expression on his face told me loud and clear: the fun was over.

I saw as his hands grab the linen handles on each side of my waist, he made eye contact with the wind controller on the outside of the dome, and nodded one time—yet another language they created. His nod began a slow decrease in the wind speed and we lowered toward the ground at the speed of, say, an elevator. I watched the top of a helper's head running on the bridge underneath us to position my wheelchair for me to drift into. It was seamless—at least that was the intention.

"Ready?" my flying man shouted over the sound of the air. I nodded my head and gave a tiny thumbs up. There was no time for any other answer, so thank God I was.

With the help of the flying man and another woman who came into the dome to help, I plopped down in my seat without complication. I, as a story chaser, would have preferred something more dramatic like a crash landing or my seat cushion bursting in flames, but everything went to plan. My hinney was back in my wheelchair and, however unnecessarily, I had two men on my trail to make sure I didn't swerve off the bridge, or just generally fall down.

"Did you have fun?" my flying instructor came from behind and asked once the wind was momentarily turned off and I could hear myself think again.

"I did," I said with all the enthusiasm I could muster. I think I heard him call me a tool, but the wind was starting back up and his voice was muted. He may have also said "cool."

I bulldozed the dome's small door open and reentered the crowd of acquaintances.

I was still smiling big and felt like I had done something special with my time, but the people in the crowd didn't return my enthusiasm. They had all either already had their turn and felt equally as special, or were waiting for their turns and were uninterested in my experience. Nobody was smiling back at me, so I rolled to the corner of the room to take off my gear.

"Hey, Kristin," a mother of a friend from the weekend's group of surfers walked over and said.

"Hey, Sharon," I said with a smile. She was one of the few in the group that I knew the name of. I first met her at a fundraiser dinner, and she shared a piece of her chicken entrée with me. To remember her name and because I'm a loony, I call her "Sharin' Sharon" in my head. It's silly, it works. With that association, I'll never forget her name or her chicken.

"I got a good picture of you while you were in there," she bragged. "You're smiling big. Look." She turned her phone screen to show me the "good" picture but, remember, there's no such thing. In place of the "good picture," I was looking at my flattened cheeks, wind-widened nostrils, and soon-to-be natty hair from the wind gusts. I looked like an alien—but not the cute, green kind with cartoon bodies. Instead, think about a combination of E.T. and the slimy one who had his head blown off in Men In Black.

"Do you want me to send it to you?" she asked.

"Yes," I said. "Yes please."

I wanted that disturbing picture sent to me because she would likely delete it from her phone after sending it, but also so I could look closer when I was alone in my car: laugh at the ugliness, then delete it from the earth.

"Thank you, Sharon," I said when my phone beeped with the picture delivery. She smiled and I faked one back to her.

"Bye," I said and scanned my eyes over the room. I said it loudly enough to blanket over both Sharin' Sharon and the group of acquaintances standing around the benches. Some of those suckers were still waiting for their turn to fly, and some were just standing around talking.

"See you," a familiar-looking man said. I smiled at him and looked into the dome one more time before bulldozing the doors of the facility and rolling out. Through the windowed door, I could see straight up the nose of a young girl flying in the air. She looked like a carved pumpkin.

Rock Climbing

The opportunity to rock climb came to me in an email from my gym. It was wintertime so the air was cold, the sky was dark, and the last thing in the world I wanted to do was leave my dog, Achilles, and the warmth of my house. But I've never adaptive rock climbed before, so I needed to try. I needed to.

"Thanks for being so patient with the setup," Adam stood over me and said. I think his name was Adam. My window of confirmation was closed, though, because already too much time had passed since his introduction. "We're almost done."

He really shouldn't have been thanking me, either—it should be the other way around. Adam and two other college-aged kids were strapping me into an elaborate harness seat so I could climb an artificial rock wall that covered an entire side of the university gym. Rock climbing in the adaptive version includes about 15 straps to wrap around my torso that filter through countless holes on my back, and a padded cushion set under my butt. Basically, we were building a flying chair.

"Not a problem," I said for maybe the third time. He kept apologizing for some reason. "Thank you, guys, for helping me. If I can make it easier, let me know." I made the same comment in three different ways every time he spoke to me so far, but it just looked so complicated. I figured the more I made the offer, the more grateful I might seem. I needed them to know I was grateful.

One of the college-aged helpers in a flannel shirt took a step in front of me and smiled.

"I love climbing," she said. "I want everybody to have the opportunity to do it." I heard her saying the same thing to a huddle of climbers behind me, so I figured it was genuine. Thank God for people like her and that mentality.

"Let me get an attachment for this," Adam held up a connector piece—as if I would be familiar, "then you'll be ready. I'll be back."

I nodded my head and held my seat on the floor, looked around. The gym was busy with people on ellipticals, weight machines, and running around an upstairs track. Most immediately around me, though, was a cluster of able-bodied men and women climbing the wall. I guessed that those were the people I would soon be climbing alongside, but who knows. Honestly, between the twenty minutes it was taking to strap me into the harness; five minutes to cram too small and not cute climbing shoes on my feet; and another five minutes of forgetting about knee pads and trying to squeeze them over said shoes, I was bored with the whole idea of climbing. Of course I wouldn't give up on it in the middle of the hour and after all the work they were doing to get me up there, but I had already decided in my head that I probably wouldn't come back in two weeks for the next climb.

"Hey," the college girl walked to me, squatted down to my eye level, and said. "Do you want some of this liquid chalk for your hands? It helps with your grip."

"Yes," I said. Chalk in liquid form—if that's a real product on the market, it sounds cool and I wanted it all over my hands.

"I use it when I climb because I get nervous and my hands sweat a lot."

"Ew?"

I didn't say that. I just smiled.

"Put a dime-sized squirt on your hand and rub it in like this," she said and frantically rubbed her hands together in front of me. It was an unnecessary display, but I appreciated it.

"Thank you," I said and took the bottle from her. I squeezed out a quarter-sized portion by accident. She didn't seem to notice.

"All right," Adam said and galloped back over to us. He was out of breath, making me think he was either very out of shape or he had to climb another wall to get the attachment strap for my costume. "Let's get this on you."

He squatted down to connect and tighten the two pieces of the harness to a loop that had another three straps coming from it. I still wasn't 100% sure how much fun this rock climbing thing would be, but at least I was confident I wouldn't fall out of my new floating chair.

"I'm going to lift you off the ground so you can start climbing," Sweaty Hand Girl stepped up and said. She was holding a thick rope connected to an axle at the top of the wall. Here, you can imagine a giant-sized pulley system with me, a lanky but smiling girl, swaying in a floating seat at the end of the rope. I was a simple machine.

She grabbed the other side of the rope and leaned her body backward for leverage, causing my seat and my body to slowly levitate off the ground. That was the fun part.

"Try to follow the trail of red rocks," she shouted from where she was standing behind me. "Those are the easiest." I nodded my head toward her and looked up at the three-story-high cluster of red, blue, and yellow plastic lumps, also called "rocks." Bring it on.

I grabbed onto the nearest red rock, to show her I was listening, and started pulling myself up the wall. Closer to the bottom, I was searching for and following the red rocks but, as I got higher, they just weren't cutting it anymore. The yellow and blue rocks are "more advanced" because they're smaller with tighter holes for my fingers, but that's the challenge I came for.

If I'm going to put on pants, leave my dog at home, and drive all the way downtown, I'm looking for a challenge. Red rocks are for beginners and, after all that time I spent sitting on the floor assembling the floating chair, I didn't feel like a beginner anymore.

The most notable challenge of rock climbing, I say with no hesitation, is the metaphoric fire that consumes my upper body before I can reach halfway. Able-bodied rock climbers can depend on their arms and legs to crawl up the rocks but, seeing as my legs don't work right now, my biceps were the stars of the show. I'm not going to call myself "out of shape," but I will confess to being "maybe not prepared" for that climb. The bicep, tricep, and scapular burn is the reason I decided to come back, though. Rock climbing requires a tedious and dependent setup procedure but, as long as those people are willing to help, I won't miss out on that burn.

––––––––

I wormed my way up the wall and toward the ceiling, pausing only for enough time to problem solve which plastic lump to grab next. Half of the thrill was feeling the fire in my body, but the other half was designing my path to the top of the wall.

"Good job, Kristin," I heard a small voice yell to me from way far below. I had gotten so preoccupied with yellow, blue, or red that I didn't see the top of the wall had snuck up to me; the ceiling of the building was in my reach. I turned my head awkwardly around and down to see the tiny bodies of Adam, I think and, unmistakably, Sweaty Hand Girl hanging on my excess rope.

"You're pretty," I heard one of the men shout. His words were barely audible so he also could have said "Are you ready?"— but I'm choosing my own adventure here.

I nodded my head to both possibilities and started to slowly descend. My arms were flopped beside me and, judging by the thumping pressure I felt on my knees, my legs were flopping underneath me. The thumping noise was indication that my knees were banging against every yellow, blue, and red rock on the way down. Thank God for those knee pads.

When I neared the ground, Sweaty Hand lowered and guided me into the seat of my parked wheelchair. Adam, accompanied by one other man I hadn't met, stepped near and started loosening straps that were now falling in front of my face and across on my chest.

"I'll give you a minute to rest, then you can go again," Adam said and added, "if you want."

"I'm ready to go now," I blurted back. I already had a solid 30 seconds in my chair. C'mon. "If you want," I added.

"Okay great. How are your knees?"

"They're good," I shot back. I honestly had no idea. I was wearing knee pads so they were probably good, right? "Let's go."

Adam and the new man re-fastened, re-tightened, and re-pulled on the straps to get me situated for another climb.

"All right," Sweaty Hand said with enthusiasm. A lot of enthusiasm. "Here we go." She pulled me into levitation above my wheelchair, and I grabbed the first red rock.

———

My second climb was smoother than the first. I didn't bother with the red lumps much, and instead followed the trail of blue. Blue lumps turned to yellow lumps, and I started feeling that beautiful burn again.

Once again, I reached the top sooner than expected. This climb wasn't as heedless as the first, though. Maybe that extra minute of rest would have been an okay idea but, in the years since my accident and with all my rehabilitation, I've adapted the unhealthy response of "I'll rest when I'm dead." This scenario didn't feel quite as dramatic as when I say it during a three-hour gym workout, but it's in the same ballpark.

When the rocks ran out and my head once again reached the gym's ceiling, I paused to catch my breath. The tiny voices were yelling to me muted from below, but I couldn't make out the words. It was likely another boy complimenting my looks, so I nodded another "thank you" and started a descent.

Again with the bangs and thumps of my knees on the rocks, and those five minutes of squeezing knee pads over my shoes were proving to be very well worth it.

I reached the bottom and, again, was lowered and guided into my wheelchair seat. A new stranger walked over and gave my liquid-chalk-and-dirt-covered hand a high five.

"You climbed that wall fast," he said. Part of me felt every second of my body's burn triple the time of my climb, but the other half believed what he said. "Do you want to go again, or are you done?" he asked. "Good job by the way."

"I'm done," I said with a little bit of relief, and a little bit of pride for standing up for my body in that way. It would have been cool to take a full minute break and try again, but I saw a few people waiting in line for my harness. "Thanks for your help."

Sweaty Hand nodded her head with a smile and one of the men looked at me with big, beautiful eyes. I think I know which of them was calling me pretty. The two of them helped unstrap me, loosen the harness, and slide the seat from under my butt.

When I took the knee pads off and inspected my body, there were five dime-sized bruises on my left knee, undeniably as result of banging on the plastic lumps while descending from the top of the wall. I didn't mind, though. They weren't particularly attractive, but it's a small price to pay.

"See you next time," Adam walked to us and said. He had an inflection in his voice that made it sound like a question, but I ignored giving the answer and smiled big in its place.

"Thank you, again," I said. I waved goodbye to a huddle of people standing over my discarded ropes on the ground, but none of them were looking in my direction. One hour ago I thought that was going to be the last time I'd see any of them again but, after a successful first climb and seeing a huddle of adorable bruises on my knee, I decided to give it another shot. If nothing else, I would come back for the man who kept calling me pretty.

Fencing

"Are you here for the clinic?" a man jumped at me from nowhere and asked.

The VA Hospital is like a maze and my face is, always has been, my biggest give away: very obviously, I was lost. Also, I'm assuming, he knew I was a visitor because nothing about my body structure or baby face suggests that I could be a veteran of anything, much less a war.

"I am," I said. "I got an email about a wheelchair fencing clinic and I'm here for it. Do you know where I go? The email said, 'multipurpose room,' but where is that?"

"Down this hallway," he smiled and pointed down the long corridor behind him. "Through the dining hall and it'll be on your left."

"Thank you," I said, smiled big, and zoomed past him. I was late.

———

Down the hallway, through the dining hall, and on my left, there were two giant, open double doors. I hurried through them and saw a group of about twenty people gathered at the opposite wall. I rolled through the door's threshold toward the crowd and gave an apologetic look to an elderly man sitting outside the group and nearest the exit. At the front of the room, where the twenty were looking, there were two people, a man and a woman close to my age, sitting in what I assumed were wheelchairs and on what I assumed was a platform.

I was assuming all of that instead of knowing it because, most notably of their outfits, they were both wearing long, gray skirts that touched the floor around them. If the clinic wasn't for *wheelchair* fencing, I might have not known they were in wheelchairs; the long skirts masked any sign of disability. I was certain that wasn't the point of the skirt, but it's a cool side effect.

On top of the gray skirt, they were wearing identical uniforms of a partially turtle necked long-sleeved jacket, and a glove on one hand. Everything was white, except for the shiny, silver swords in their hands.

Most notably, the swords in their hands.

They looked exactly like I thought they would look, that is, exactly like they do in the movies. The guard, a silver shield covering the sword's handle, was about as big as my open hand; the blade was skinny and long; and the whole thing looked like it weighed less than one pound. Their swords were connected to a wire that was connected to a box on the ground at their side. It was a lot to take in.

"I'm late," everyone turned to look at me as I entered their huddle, so I confirmed. I decided to own it, not apologize for it. The clock on the wall read 4:33 PM so I was only three minutes late, but it felt like I missed the whole introduction.

"That's okay," a familiar face stepped beside me and said. I vaguely recognized her from my time interning in the research lab in the VA Hospital when I was in college, but no name came to mind. In my defense, I was working under a grant program that only lasted a few months, so my time was brief. "I'm glad you came. We're going over the different types of weapons: *epee, sabre, and foil. We're passing some around for you to hold.*"

I nodded my head and said, "thank you," as if I understood one word of her jargon. I did see the swords being passed, though, so I moved my chair to park next to a friendly-looking blonde girl with the first sword, apparently called "epee," in her hands.

"Here you go," she said, seconds after I parked next to her. She placed the sword into my open palms. It could have been a scene from King Arthur, except I wasn't going to bow my head as I received it from her. That would have been weird.

I rolled the sword around in my hands and felt how light it was. That, at least, I was right about. The handle of the sword, sticking out from under the guard, was also what I imagined: as long as my full hand and not differing from the handle of a squirt gun. The tip of the three-foot-long blade has a rubber ball over it that's about the size of a blueberry. The swords weren't scary-looking to me but, if they were, I imagine the blueberry tips would take away some of that fear.

I passed it along the line, and my blonde friend handed me two more swords to hold, both with different handles. The first handle looked just like a pole, and just like I've seen in the movies. That, I learned from the man at the front of the group that was talking in my background, is called a French grip. The second sword, he said, had what's called a pistol grip: hard, metal bumps sticking from its handle, meant to guide the fencer's fingers to regulation. The finger position is a little complicated because it required my thumb to overlap pointer finger, middle finger over ring finger, hand on head, leg in the air. Something like that. I passed the sword along to the woman next to me before it got too frustrating.

"So there are three different kinds of weapons," the man in the front announced to our group, "and today we're going to fight with the one you held. The epee. The other weapons are called foil and sabre. They're all a little different, but epee is the easiest to learn."

"My partner and I will fight a five-point bout to show you what it looks like," he continued and nodded at the girl, who remained quiet until that moment.

"Five hits equal five points," she said. I still kind of felt like everyone else understood these concepts better than I did, but I was faking it with a head nod.

Flashback to college.

"In a bout of epee, you only get a point if you hit your opponent with the tip of the blade." By 'the tip,' she meant the blueberry. "If you hit your opponent with the side of the blade, no point is scored, and the bout goes on." She put a finger on the blueberry. "There's a sensor on the tip that'll detect when you've scored a point." She held up the wire that was connecting her weapon to the box on the ground, then continued. "When you score, the sensor goes off and this box will beep at you." She looked at the box and then to her audience with satisfaction that I recognized.

"We wear masks that cover our head and neck for protection," she said. "Getting hit without it hurts a lot." She gave us a meaningful look that made me think she was probably talking from experience. Noted.

As if on cue, she and the man in the chair opposite her locked eyes and picked up their clunky masks from the ground. With one well-practiced motion, they slid them over their faces and all features were lost. The masks reminded me of the ones beekeepers wear, except the fencing version covered the entire head and neck, instead of just the face. They looked fierce, and I wanted one.

"Okay," a new woman walked in front of the demonstrators and said. She looked like someone in charge—maybe a coach. "I'll give the signal and they'll fence a couple of bouts for you." She turned around to face the fencers and they raised their weapons. "En garde."

The man and woman set their arms at hip level and lifted their weapons to cross in the middle. They hovered in that spot for a second or two before the coach spoke again. "Ready... Fence."

The millisecond following her command, the demonstrators started moving in their seats like worms, avoiding the poke of their opponent's blueberry. With all that movement, I noticed metal handlebars positioned over their wheelchair's tires opposite their fencing arm, providing support and lunge ability to their wiggling bodies. That bar answered my question of how they were able to move around so freely without faceplanting on the auditorium floor. With the generally diminished core strength that's almost consistent among paralyzed athletes, I can assure you that kind of movement wouldn't be possible without the bar.

While their bodies wormed around, their swords were hitting each other with loud, clanging noises. It was beautifully dramatic. Often one of them would lunge at the other, trying to squish the blueberry on the other person's body. A couple of bounced and deflected sword hits on the woman, and I realized she was wearing a chest protector. That's smart, and also a "duh."

"Notice how they're using the bar to dodge the blade," the coach narrated, "but also lunging to make contact with their opponent." The buzzer sounded, indicating the man scoring a point on the girl's shoulder. "You can only be hit above the waist because the sensor doesn't pick up contact on the skirt."

"Oh," I said, kind of loudly. "I thought they were wearing those to look cute."

At the time it felt like a funny comment, but I regretted it as soon as I finished. It just wasn't funny. The man gave me a small laugh and pulled up his skirt. He was wearing pants underneath, of course, and I saw that his legs were held together at the thighs by a thick, cloth strap.

"That's also a reason we wear them," he said with a smile. He was playing along with my weird humor, which I appreciated. "I like the way it looks on me."

Bless his heart.

"These two are going to transfer back into their normal chairs and let you guys try," the coach said and added, "if you want to." She looked at the group of us eagerly. "Who wants to try?"

Surprisingly, only four people from the group of twenty wanted to fence. Not surprisingly, my hand was the first in the air.

"Great," she said and looked at the small group of volunteers. Her expression showed no disappointment at the small number, but I wondered why those people bothered to come to a fencing demonstration and not want to try it? It doesn't make sense to me. "My name is Jen. Come to the side of the stage and put on some protection."

I looked to the side stage at the giant pile of white clothing, helmets, and other equipment I didn't know the name of yet. Despite my immediacy in volunteering, I didn't feel much excitement, but rather a reluctance. I just washed my hair and didn't want to catch other people's helmet germs, the turtleneck jacket and chest protector were likely covered in dried stranger sweat, the glove looked like it had been used for years and years without a wash, and my list of hygiene-related paranoias goes on.

Contrary, I used gas money to drive here and took time out of my night to come, so I rolled over to the side stage. Despite my list of hesitations, I was still the first to move toward it.

The woman in charge skipped over and dropped a pile of clothes in my lap as soon as I was in drop distance, as if I even remotely knew what I was doing. I saw the long-sleeved jacket on top; a vertically-halved shirt with short sleeves; and a hard, plastic shield to wear for a chest protector. Again, everything white.

"I'll help you get these on," Jen looked at me and said. "Have you ever fenced before?"

"I haven't," I said. And, to add to my forced enthusiasm, "It looks like a lot of fun, though."

"A lot of fun" is a little bit of a stretch, but Jen's response was a giant smile, so it was good.

"I watched you during the demonstration and saw a sparkle in your eye," she said. "I can tell you're going to be good at this."

It's not clear if she really saw the sparkle or she saw me after I yawned and my eyes watered, but her energy was rubbing off; I was getting into this fencing thing. Or, at least, the idea of it. For the most part, say something nice to me and I'll fall into the corresponding role or characteristic, no matter what it is. I'm very easily peer pressured, at least I realize it.

Jen waved her hand for me to put on the chest protector, half shirt, and jacket that was on my lap. She picked up the one glove and explained that I should wear it on my dominant hand, the one holding my weapon.

I did as I was told, outfitting myself in a full fencing costume. Once I was fully suited up, I noted that the shirts and glove felt clean and freshly washed. Much appreciation to those folks—we all know how worried I was about that.

"Try on this mask," Jen said and handed me the beekeeping mask. It weighed about two pounds and looked absolutely silly. Even still, the mask, from what I could tell, is the coolest part of the sport.

"If you like this and want to compete, we travel around the world for tournaments," she said. That word, travel, is all you really need to say to get me on board. "The qualifying match last year was in Anaheim, California. There's a camp in Montreal, the trials are in Italy, then, if you do well, the Paralympics are in Paris." She motioned toward the demonstrators behind me. "He has been to the Paralympics twice and she's a hopeful."

Jen said all the keywords: travel, California, and Paralympics. Now I really had a sparkle.

Jen and I talked for ten more minutes while I waited for my turn to fence. By the time my name was called to roll onto the platform and put my wheelchair into position, my impulse and "yes" habit had verbally committed me to not only the sport, but to try for a spot on the national team, and to compete for the chance to represent my country in the Paralympics.

Thank God for that sparkle in my eye, ya know? It was giving Jen all the foundationless confidence she could handle.

"You're up, girl," Jen said. "Transfer into that wheelchair and we'll get you strapped in." She pointed to a taller, more unstable-looking chair sitting on a platform.

I nodded my head twice then rolled my wheelchair onto the platform, next to the new chair. I transferred on, Jen whisked my wheelchair from the stand, and I spent 30 more seconds wiggling around in the foreign seat cushion until I felt close to comfortable.

Then, I turned my head sideways to face my beekeeping opponent. I couldn't even recognize the gender of the person I was about to fence, but it didn't matter much. We were both ready to go.

I thought the clothes were clean and fresh when I put them on but, judging by how hot I was after fifteen minutes of waiting my turn, I wasn't so confident. Combine that sweat with the heat of my face in that mask, and fencing is not a sport for first dates. I'm not sure why anyone would want to fence on a first date, but I'm confirming that it is not a good idea.

"En garde," came the familiar command for the beginning of the bout. We both raised our weapons at hip level to cross in midair, just like the demonstration, and hovered for about three more seconds before "Ready…Fence."

Both of us wiggled around, supported by the metal bar over our wheel, and tried to poke the other with our blueberries. I don't want you to imagine this as a long or even legitimate-feeling battle; each bout lasted less than five seconds before one of us scored a point. I'm also saying that "one of us scored a point" like it wasn't me every time, but don't let me fool you. I am not a natural.

Needless to say, the first five-point bout kicked my butt: I think the score was 1-5. The next bout, though, I did well and landed most of my pokes. I don't know why I temporarily improved, but it could have been out of my opponent's pity. Either way, my success didn't carry to the next bout, as it was like my first. Actually, in the wake of my promise to "go to the Paralympics, for sure," I was pretty disappointed to not be naturally expert.

"Good job, girl," Jen walked from nowhere and said. I was hoping she went to the bathroom and missed me completely because I prefer her confidence to be foundationless and based solely on my enthusiasm. "You're a natural."

"Did you see me, though?" I asked. My hand hurt from my death grip on the sword handle and I was feeling humbled.

"I did," she said. "It's only your first time, Kristin. You just need practice." She either winked at me or blinked very hard, I couldn't tell.

Fencing, a peculiar sport I initially wrote off because of my small frame and borderline oversensitive personality, was kind of fun and maybe something I could learn to love. Again, power of the compliment. I didn't expect to like it and I didn't expect to want to get better at it, but I did. I like it and I want to be good.

"We'll be in touch," Jen confirmed. She tuned me back to the conversation. "I'll see what I can do about getting you a coach in Richmond. We need to get you ready for the qualifiers."

I nodded my head and smiled—genuinely smiled. I'm well trained in both fake smiling and being a "yes" girl, but this time was real. Especially because she said I have a shot at going to the Paralympics one day, I was sold. I really will do almost anything for an excuse to travel.

Jen was true to her word and, the following week, I began private lessons at a fencing club in my city. My fencing master, Walter, is committed to making my dream come true. I practice four to five days a week, own most of my own equipment, and have justification to not only leave swords on the floor of my living room, but to wear that beekeeping mask whenever I feel like it.

Later that year, my enthusiasm from the clinic materialized into an invitation to train at the Olympic Training Center in Colorado Springs for one week with Paralympians, whom I can now call my friends. I've qualified for attended in North American Cups held around the country, and I've placed in the top five at all of them. I still have the dream of representing my country in the Paralympics—a dream born from my impulse and being caught up in the moments of the clinic.

Wheelchair fencing, most affectionally called Parafencing, gives me an edge that I otherwise lack—remember "borderline oversensitive." This time, my impulse led me to great things and big dreams. With the support of my family, the opportunity of the sport, and a new set of local and national fencing friends, I fell in love with it and I'm working my hardest to be the best.

The Downside

I 've made this disability seem fun, and most of the time it is for me. Really. I'm happy to cast a different light on a situation that seems hard and sad. Paralysis has opened a lot of doors and it has given me perspective and maturity that I wouldn't trade for a mountain of gold.

There is a downside to all of this, though, and that probably comes as no surprise. In addition to the obvious bummer of not being able to walk or to play on a regular sports team, there's a handful, two handfuls, of things I have to incorporate into my everyday life in order to maintain a "normal" lifestyle. More simply put: there's a lot going on behind the scenes.

On top of my own list of setbacks is wounds. Unfortunately, the cost of my staying active is also the biggest reason for my skin breakdown. I struggle a lot with this. Before my accident and since as far back as I can remember, I've been active on sports teams, running around the neighborhood after school, and even being crowned captain of my lacrosse team as a high school freshman. Then the Jet Ski hit me, I lost mobility in my lower extremities, and what I thought was all my athleticism. My heart broke—it absolutely broke.

About six months after being discharged from the hospital, I discovered and fell in love with my first adaptive sport: skiing. Since then, I've tried every sport available to me in its adaptive form (14 and counting) in a fight to hold on to this outlet I've had since I was a kid. Not only that, I now have a body that doesn't get the same thoughtless exercise that able-bodied people do with walking. That just means I have to be extra conscious to not let my belly poof out like so many stereotypes suggest.

That's the reasoning behind my drive to get out of my house and risk it, but here we come to the consequence: pressure sores. They really get me. A normally-feeling person's mind and body work together to, for the most part, keep pressure sores at bay. Normal people have the subconscious instinct to move around, unweight, and readjust when pressure is applied to the skin for extended periods of time, therefore evading skin breakdown and wound development. My body, with its distorted brain signals and perpetual ambiguity, is not privileged to those subconscious messages. Again with the awareness, I have to be one step ahead of this issue at all times, or else I'll get a wound. I've learned that the hard way: the weeping, bleeding, and slow-healing hard way.

But the wounds—they're worth it, right? Right. They're a price I haven't yet figured out how to not have to pay. It would be easier to sit at home and likely be free from them, yes, but that poof. I'm fighting the poof.

My physical therapist in the hospital used to chant at me "just because you can't feel it doesn't mean it's not there, Kristin" what seemed like every time I looked her way. I didn't like physical therapy or being an inpatient in the hospital and she was unfortunately bundled into that dislike, so I wanted to roll over her toe every time she said it. Very soon I realized that the meaning of her words, awareness, held the most important lesson I learned. Again, the hard way.

Did my foot fall off the footplate? If so, it could get caught under my wheels and I could break my ankle. I can't feel my legs, but I need to know where they are at all times if I want to keep my already-weakening bones intact.

When was the last time I resituated in my seat? Sitting in the same spot for a long time is uncomfortable for a normal person, cue those subconscious movements, so I need to make sure to periodically relieve pressure on my butt, so a wound won't form. I'm sure I don't have to convince anyone that a wound on the butt of someone in a wheelchair is literally the most inconvenient thing.

Is there anything touching my lower body while I sleep? The constant pressure for an extended period of time, like during the night, is not inconsequential. Since I can't feel discomfort from the constant pressure, I won't adjust to prevent my skin from breaking down, resulting in a very annoying surprise when I wake in the morning.

Is the surface I sit on too hard? As much as I'd like to claim to having a butt like Beyoncé, it just isn't true. Spinal cord injury not only took some movement and feeling from me, it also stole a lot of the butt muscle I worked so hard to build. What I'm left with is a bony butt that's overly sensitive to a lack of cushion underneath. I have to protect the skin that covers those bones, since my muscles don't exist to do the job.

Where is that streak of blood on the ground coming from? I must stop everything and check my whole lower body until I find an origin. The usual culprit is an impaired toe, but I've learned to never underestimate the possibility of spewed blood from my calf, ankle, or knee.

Similar story for a dot or patch of blood on the fabric of sheets, clothes, carpet, and on my leather couch. As consequence, I've become an expert at getting blood out of almost anything. And if I can't scrub it out, I have a hall closet stocked with stain removing products to help.

These are just a few examples off a longer list of things I've trained myself to be aware of and, honestly, sometimes force myself to care about. There comes a rare time I want to throw my hands up and say "Too much! I'm staying inside this week!" It's rare and only lasts a hot second, but it has happened before. Those though0ts lose their steam with the always lingering comparison to others with my similar disability. The best way to take all the fun out of giving up on something is to compare myself to those people with chronic pain, who lost the ability to get out of the house as easily as I can; quadriplegics, who don't have use of their arms; or amputees, who might not even have arms. Again, few examples off a long list.

I feel very fortunate in my disability and it's pretty cool to have access to adaptive sports, but it all comes with a price. In this case, **it ain't cheap**.

Speaking of "cheap," it really isn't. Between the cost of wound care supplies, which we've learned I always need, and the equipment necessary for me to just get through the day, paralysis is an extremely expensive predicament to be in. Aside from those supplies, I have a short but expensive list of medical necessities—only partially covered by insurance.

When I say that "my disability ain't cheap," I'm speaking about to the outrageous cost of keeping myself healthy and rehabilitating my body. This list includes, but is certainly not limited to, therapy outside of the inpatient hospital (the hourly rate alone is shocking); equipment to maintain my health as much as I can (a standing frame to support my bones and an FES bike to strengthen muscles); and extracurricular equipment in its adaptive form (handcycle to compete in marathons and a special wheelchair for fencing in tournaments). Insurance helps a little by partially covering the cost of medical equipment, but all the extras they won't touch with a 39 ½ foot pole. No way. God forbid someone has a dream of regaining sensation and/or movement below their injury level like I do. I can spend some fast and serious money with my big dreams. It doesn't seem fair.

But then again, neither is life. Moving on.

Accessibility is a huge factor, as you might imagine. On top of the overall inaccessibility of the city I live in, bathrooms that are almost consistently too tight to squeeze into, and the assumption that I'll need to be airlifted up the steps to anyone

I visit, where I'm going to live is another hurdle to jump. Like most, I moved back into my parents' house after I graduated from college. My parents are very fun people and I had a great time living with them again as an adult, but I eventually had the idea for my own space.

It took me a couple of years to have that idea, remember "very fun," but I began a search for one story, single-family homes in or around my city of Richmond, Virginia. I can't tell you how many houses I visited in the months following, mostly because they all blur together into one big "*NO*," but I can guarantee you it was a lot. Don't get me wrong—I fell in love with almost every one of them. I also can't tell you how many times I called my mom to say I'd found The One.

With every One I found, literally all of them required some kind of major renovation before I was able to move in: a high majority needed widened doorways, and every single One needed a wheelchair-accessible renovation to the bathroom. In a few, I even tried to compromise by saying that I didn't need to be able to fit my chair in the guest bathroom because "I'll never go in there anyway. I think this is The One."

Thank God for my parents' interference in this situation because I didn't buy any of those Ones. In the end, I found a reasonably priced lot and built my dream house for me and Achilles. Everything is accessible, I can get into and spin around in every bathroom, and it doesn't scream "*WHEELCHAIR*" in the way that an old house with new accessibility renovations would. My house is reasonably sized, normal looking, and a perfectly accessible space for me and my beautiful dog.

The combination of the cost of living, accessibility, and dreaming beyond this wheelchair results in an expensive disposition. As you can see, **it ain't reasonable**.

Bladder control, or lack thereof, is something else to consider. If you'll allow me to be the most vulnerable with you, I'll share a little on this topic.

The loss of control and sensation in my bladder is the biggest consequence of my disability. By this point I have a solid routine for managing that loss and it doesn't interfere so much with my everyday life, but it hasn't always been that way. In high school, the years I was first injured, I was learning not only how to manage my newly paralyzed body, but also my "new" bladder. My accident took from me the ability to read its messages ("I have to pee"), suppress it ("I can hold it until I find a bathroom"), or completely void it (here starts the UTIs).

Oh, the [embarrassing] stories I have.

My lack of sensation for when I have to go to the bathroom means I empty my bladder on a schedule, every four hours to be exact. Once I was out of the hospital and managing my own bladder routine, for a long time I felt stuck. I would go to the bathroom and, knowing I had only four hours until I had to find an accessible bathroom to go again, I would almost literally count down the minutes; my thoughts and actions started to revolve around bathroom breaks. Along with adding stress and taking the fun out of leaving my house and its accessibility, it was exhausting.

Time went on and I learned to relax into my paralysis. My body has created a new language for telling me when something is going on and, with years of trial and error, I can read it almost fluently. I might not have normal sensation related to a full bladder, but I'm fortunate enough to have a body that tells me in other ways: sometimes that looks like spasms from my hips and sometimes my left foot points to lift my leg. I'm not confident enough to depend on those alternative messages—I still stick to a somewhat consistent schedule—but I fully recognize how fortunate I am to have a body that's trying to wake up for me.

This is all just a peek into the most inconvenient and complicated aspect of a life with paralysis. I didn't even touch on the embarrassment and shame that comes with having a bladder accident, as an adult woman, in public. Those occurrences are rare now, thanks Jesus, and I don't imagine you need to be convinced that it's awful—absolutely awful.

I think I've armed you with enough knowledge to empathize with me here: losing bladder control? **It ain't easy**.

So now we've learned that disability is expensive with regard to money and health; unreasonably priced in necessity and accessory; and problematic, both socially and logistically. I can think of many more adjectives to pin to this subset of my disability, but those are at the top of the list.

I'm not sure exactly what I'm trying to say here, other than "it's not as easy as it seems." Living with and being confined (for now) to a wheelchair probably doesn't seem easy, but I want to be extra sure I'm not depicting it as such. Like I said, I'm extremely fortunate in my disability because of the abilities I do still have, the community that surrounds and supports me, and the fire under my butt that keeps me fighting every day toward my dreams of walking again.

Promise

"Beep...beep...beep...beep...beep"

When you're lying in a hospital bed all day, it feels like a machine of some sort is always sounding off. My antibiotic sessions last anywhere from one to three hours, and those hours collapse into brief reprieves until the bags reach empty and the machines start beeping, beeping away my sanity.

Similar to the bladder control predicament I spoke of last chapter, I began to spend my days in countdown for the end of the IV treatments—when the beeping would start.

Nurses don't hear the racket of the IV machines, and that's universal. At the first hospital I stayed in, a trauma center near our rented vacation home in Florida, the nurses simply ignored it. They ignored call light beeps, IV completion beeps, and maybe even if I screamed "BEEP" as loud as I could. In their defense, because someone needs to be, maybe they just don't hear them anymore.

I can empathize by way of my parents' old house next to the interstate. Anyone visiting said the noise of cars was in the foreground but, because it was in my constant background, I had to focus to hear it at all. In the same way, the nurses seem to grow immune to the beeps, but I don't think I ever will.

One nurse, bless her, taught me how to "system off" the machines, taking away all chance for incessant noise while I wait for a hospital staff member to rescue me. I'm not completely sure what I'm doing and one of these days I'll mess up an IV treatment by turning the machine off before it's complete, but that's a chance I'm willing to take. Turning it off also takes away its opportunity to tell me if something is wrong, i.e. do its job, so there's my second risk. Both are highly unnecessary risks, but worth it for the reward of peace, right? Not really.

———

"Can I help you?" a muffled, male voice penetrated my newly beep-free hospital room. His voice was coming from the speaker on the dual tv remote/call button attached to my bed rail. I pushed the "Call" button a solid seven minutes ago and before my fumble-then-shutdown of the IV machine. With that delay, I was sure to either be dead, or accepting of my new life alongside the problem. In this case, the latter.

"Will you send my nurse in?" I asked in my attempt at a very sweet voice. I've read the studies on attractive people getting extra care and attention at these places, so I wanted the man at the switchboard to know me as The Sweet-Sounding Girl in Room 112. Maybe then he would prioritize my requests.

Clearly, I had a lot of time to overthink things.

No further acknowledgment from my friend in the box, but I did hear a click from the other side. That click meant he hung up his phone without a "thanks, cutie," "talk to ya later, sweetheart," nothing. I had more work to do.

"What's going on in here?" a middle-aged woman with long, blonde hair opened my door one minute later and asked. They never knock, but that's something I got used to. She showed up uncharacteristically quickly, so I was impressed enough to excuse an abrupt entrance.

"I think my antibiotic is finished," I said, again with my sweet voice. This is a game. "I turned the machine off to stop the beeping."

"Okay," she said and took three strides to my bedside. "You turned it off—good girl. That noise will drive you crazy." Positive reinforcement for my uninformed, yet executive decisions. Yes, I will keep doing it and yes, this nurse just jumped to the top of my short list of favorites." Let's get you unhooked," she finished the journey to the IV machine next to my head, pushed a few buttons, and started sanitizing to disconnect my line. "I'll give your next antibiotic in about an hour. Give your body a little break."

"Great," I said. Lying in bed all day and being dependent on other people for everything outside of my short reach meant that I was very cooperative. I felt like a baby. A cute baby who gets extra attention from the staff for being so cute, but still a baby. "Thanks for your help."

She winked at me and shuffled out of my room, likely straight into another patient's room.

God bless the nurses, ya know?

———

The reason I was at Promise Hospital, allow me to get personal again, is because of a wound on my butt. Wounds are easy to develop on the ischial bone ("sit bone") of a wheelchair user, as result of constant pressure and a lack of frequent weight shifting or unloading. Also, to reiterate, they're awful.

In this case, I had a wound on my ischium with significant depth. Instead of slowing down and spending a majority of my time on the couch with zero butt-surface contact, I decided it would be okay to do a marathon; go to the Olympic Training Center in Colorado and wheelchair fence for a week; practice and compete for two seasons of adaptive rowing; and chase balls around a tennis court for two seasons of wheelchair tennis. No surprise to anyone, the wound got deeper, and I paid the price. Duh, Kristin.

I had to have surgery to close it up and clear the infection, which I picked up from who knows which activity and who knows how early into the breakdown. It was pretty scary and very serious. To reiterate, there are 1,000 products on the market for helping heal a wound, but the most inconvenient yet most effective cure is zero pressure, one hundred percent of the time. It's awful.

That looks like: lying in bed all day. Also, that most likely looks like: lying in a hospital bed all day. Because let's be honest—if I was at home, I would be too tempted to get up in my wheelchair and roll around. Given the ability to cheat, I just don't think I could stay out of my chair.

So, I moved into the hospital. More accurately, I moved into a bed in the hospital. I went to the bathroom while lying in bed, took a shower while lying in bed, ate all meals while lying in bed, and checked my social media while lying in bed. In those four weeks, I was up to date on the prosaic details of my friends' everyday life via social media more than I ever wanted to have time to be.

In the vein of playing my tiny violin, let's talk about this bed I spent so much time in. I was sleeping on a cloud, and not in a good way. There's a special mattress, made of sand and air, that's specifically good for promoting healing in pressure sores. The sand and air are trapped in large bubbles and positioned over what I imagine is a large blower, because my body was constantly moving with the pressure of the blows. Lying in that bed felt like a weak version of those electric massage chairs in the middle of malls that you waste something like $3 on. In the mattress version, though, it feels less like a massage and more like hundreds of pillow people trapped inside the bubbles and banging on the ceiling, my body, with their pillow fists. By the nature of the cloud mattress, it provides absolutely no support on my back, shoulders, or spine. Hey, painful. Also, my doctor told me those beds cost the hospital upwards of $140,000 and they break frequently.

Moving on.

———

In every hospital I've stayed in or visited, there has always been at least three or four nurses that shouldn't be nurses. Those are the names I pray to not see written under the "Care Team" section of my room's whiteboard. My displeasure is backed up by the fact of them being rude, distracted, or they just didn't give me confidence in being under their care.

This particular hospital, though, was different; I liked all the nurses. For this particular wound, I was trapped there for four weeks, so being in good favor with the hospital staff is a make-it-or-break-it for me not going loony.

I think the "long term care" status of the hospital had a lot to do with the quality of the nursing staff. "Long term care" means there were fewer patients, so a lighter load for the nurses; the hallways were almost completely quiet, void of the occasional moan from an older-sounding victim; the cafeteria didn't have to feed a large number of patients, resulting in consistently tolerable meals; and every patient had a private room with mediocre picture quality on the televisions.

I'm making this all sound great and, to be fair, it was pretty cool as far as hospitals go. But you guys are smarter than to think it was that enchanting.

Remember: it's still a hospital.

There are still machines that sound off, the nurses still poke their heads in my room at all hours of the night, and, lest we forget, there's still a wound on my butt that forced its way into the nucleus of my thoughts.

———

"Hey, girl," a familiar nurse banged into my room and said. She walked straight to my bedside and looked into a clear, plastic box hanging off the end of my bed. "You haven't been drinking much today. I'll get you some water."

"Thank you," I said to the back of her head walking out of the room. I doubt my agreement or inclinations mattered much at this point but, just in case she could hear me, manners.

I learned early into my stay that everything goes smoother if I surrender my humility, privacy, independence, desire to maintain muscle mass in my body, and thirst for the outside elements very early on. My first and biggest slap in perspective came when they started monitoring and commenting on my urine output by way of that plastic box at the end of my bed. My cape of normalcy was torn off pretty quickly after arriving here.

Making those sacrifices are a lot harder than they sound, and they don't even sound easy. If you refuse or are hesitant to surrender any of those things, your stay in the hospital is going to be a little, probably a lot, tough. There's nothing better than being an inpatient to give you a kick of humility and make you appreciate all the otherwise insignificant aspects of your life, am I right?

An example of the time before my acceptance came during the first week of my stay. I had to call a nurse to my room to help me clean up a mess on my body and, because I hadn't completely gone through that list, I was still in a phase of feeling embarrassed for my dependence on others. In hindsight it's silly, but my shame felt very real in that moment. The nurse didn't seem completely thrilled about having to help me, either; she had her Work Face on, where I needed her to have her Smiley Face on while she worked.

I laid there watching her clean up the mess and, because I am becoming my mother, I cried. My tears weren't exclusive to this one mess-and-clean-up incident, mind you, but more for the overall lack of independence I was still accepting. I said "you have to surrender" those things like it's quick and easy, but please understand it is a process.

I'm trying to make this next part not sound so manipulative of me, but there's really no way around it.

The nurse started to console me and, in that consoling, she became soft. So I kept crying. It was a silent cry, but that was all it took to hold her sympathy until the job was done. Now, instead of leaving with a scowl, she left with a "Bless you, sweetie. I hope you get better."

I should get an award for this.

————

"Is tonight Hair Night?" Mom asked. Every day, she and Dad came to visit me after playing pickleball or going to an art class. I had trouble convincing them to spend their vacation doing something more fun than sitting in a hospital room with me, but they're a tough sell.

"It sure is," I said and smiled so big at her. It really was Hair Night, but I might have said "yes" no matter what; washing my hair was the most exciting activity of my days in there. When I'm stuck lying in a hospital bed, "Hair Night" looked like Mom shampooing her hands and giving me a head massage.

Even though I literally stayed in the same spot all day long—a spot nowhere near the dirt of the outside—I managed to feel just as gross as I do on a normal day in the world. It's all in my head, clearly. Pun intended.

"I'll ask one of the nurses for a trash can and some towels," she said and motioned toward the Call button on my bed's remote.

If you weren't already convinced of my fortune on these nights, I'll get you with the description of our process.

Mom takes the rail off the side of my bed, we pile towels underneath my neck to catch flyaway water-soak, and I twist my body into a painful "C" to dangle over the side. She fills a hospital tub with warm water; positions the trash can below my mane; and proceeds to scrub, rinse, and shake until my hair is clean. Then, she wraps it in a towel, combs out the knots, and blows it dry with a hairdryer brought from home. If I close my eyes and manage to forget where I am, I might think I was at a spa.

I'm kidding. It's impossible to forget where I am: I'm stuck on a vibrating balloon with an IV-line dangling from my arm.

Again, we're moving on.

———

"Thank you, Mom," I said when my hair was rinsed and clean. I moved my body from the "C" shape to a more comfortable "b" with my back flat on the mattress and my legs twisted to the right. While I changed letters, Mom wound my hair tightly in a towel and guided my head back to my pillow. This is our routine.

Having clean hair made me feel prettier, but I'm fully aware that "pretty" has a glass ceiling when you're an inpatient. I'm only as attractive as my hospital robe, and this one was covered in blue triangles and did not cover my butt crack.

"Look how pretty your hair is," Mom said and handed me the mirror from my side table.

"I look like a fat baby boy," I said and dramatically returned it to the table. I brought a mirror from home so I could monitor my overgrown eyebrows and dry skin flakes on my face. Gross, but it's like a car accident. I just wanted to look.

"You're beautiful," she said. Clearly, she is my mother. A mother is the only person who would call her adult daughter, who looks like an overweight male infant, "beautiful."

"Lay there for a minute and I'll dry your hair," she continued, "after I get the knots out."

This part is definitely not like a spa; Bedrest Tangles are no joke. I'm not aware I'm doing it but, apparently, I swish around on my bed pillow enough to create an almost literal rat's nest in the back of my head. Suffice to say, the otherwise relaxing circumstance of someone combing and styling my hair is completely nonexistent here. I'll even go as far as to say that if I didn't have Mom to wash and comb me every few days, I would give myself a bob haircut with little hesitation.

Maybe I'm being a little dramatic, but not much. Have you ever been poked in the belly with a kitchen knife? I'm not saying it's the same pain, but it's close.

She told me to "turn your head this way" and "turn your head the other way" to the tune of my cringing face, until the comb finally ran through my hair without stopping.

"Good grief," I said as soon as she returned the comb to its place on my nightstand. She went straight into pushing through her bag for the hairdryer, pulled both the dryer and an ever-long cord from it, then plugged it into the socket above my head.

Another round and another five minutes of "turn your head this way" and "turn your head the other way," and I was the happiest girl I know. It's amazing how positive of a difference a clean head of hair makes, even in places as uninspiring as a hospital. Also, drying implicated absolutely no pain or discomfort, whereas detangling brought it all. As long as the mirror is on the other side of the room, I'm the happiest girl.

"Thank you so much," I said, my voice in unbroken exhale.

"I'm happy to do it," she said and handed me my cell phone. "You got a text message."

This was exciting to me. It's easy to believe when I say that the hospital is an extremely isolating place; I felt like people forgot about me. The feeling is similar to when I was in high school and college in the years after my accident. I had such a contrasting lifestyle from my peers: in high school, they were getting their driver's licenses and dressing up for homecoming while I was relearning how to go to the bathroom and pull up my pants on my own. In college, I was traveling to California for rehab and the Dominican Republic for stem cell injections, while they were binge drinking and having casual sex. In this case, I was lying on my side in a hospital bed 24 hours a day, while my friends were going to work and having a say in what they ate for dinner. I felt very much on the outside.

So, you see my reason, a text message from a friend at home is a highlight.

"Thanks," I said and looked at my phone's screen.

The text message was from my bank, informing me of a withdrawal for my credit card statement. My bank. I deflated.

Lying in the bed with internet connection is a dangerous thing for me, Ms. Impulsive eBay Shopper. Earlier that morning I won three bids for three pairs of socks, a toothbrush, and a koala costume—all for Achilles. I'm very impulsive, but also a very Crazy Dog Mom.

I didn't necessarily want to admit my purchases to Mom, or that the text was from my bank instead of a friend checking in on me, so I was silent.

"I wonder what Paul does in his free time," I said, changing the subject after another minute. She looked at me, understandably confused. It may have seemed out of the blue, but I had time to think in there.

"What made you think of that?" she asked.

"I'm not sure," I said. I did wonder about the answer, but there was more to cover. "But I haven't talked to Megan in eight months. I don't think we're friends anymore."

Mom laughed and turned back to look at her phone screen, but we both knew I was right.

———

I spent four total weeks at Promise and, nearing the end, I had a rapport with nearly all of the nurses. Our friendships were enough that they would often stop by my room just to say "hello," see how my day was going, and/or give update on something we talked about in times earlier. I was told that I was the youngest and most coherent patient on my floor, so that probably had something to do with their enthusiasm. One Night Nurse with a particularly low voice made habit of stopping in to chat at two or three o'clock in the morning, which I eventually got used to.

Some days it felt like I would never get out of there, and some days it felt okay. Honestly, most days were numb; a cycle of Mom, Dad, and my grandfather came to "sit with" me day in and day out, which was helpful. That looked like: a lot of card games, a lot of HGTV, and The Bachelor every Monday night. That part I loved.

———

The end of my hospital term did finally come, though, which meant I was getting out of there. I was getting out, but not before I relearned how to sit up. Or, at least, convince my surgeon I knew how to sit up.

"You can sit for 15 minutes today," he explained. "Tomorrow you can have 30 minutes, then 45, and keep adding 15 minutes until you reach 90."

"Got it," I said. It felt like the best days of my life were ahead of me. My day of discharge was contingent on the success of my sitting, so I was determined to get it right. I decided then that, despite the progression being extremely tedious, I wasn't going to cheat; I would sit for my allotted minutes then get back in bed, no matter what kind of exciting upright tooth brushing or vertical meal eating I was in the middle of.

"Do you want to sit up now or while you eat dinner?" Mom asked.

"Right now," I said with a smile. "I've been waiting four weeks for this, so I don't want to waste it on dinner."

"Okay," she said. "I'll help you get off this mattress."

Usually, I can get off the mattress by myself with ease, but I didn't know what to expect with regards to my possible lightheadedness and my possible deficit in core strength. I've been bedbound before and those were two of the most annoying side effects. At Promise, I was more proactive by way of free weights and a TheraBand, but there's no telling how big or little difference that made. Mom lifted my shrunken body off the mattress balloon and set me down in my seat.

"Okay," I said, cautiously after a minute of sitting. "This isn't hard." Thank God, sitting upright wasn't as dramatic as I thought. Contrary, it was nothing but fun.

I rolled to the bathroom and brushed my teeth in the sink vs. laying down and trying not to drool on my chest; washed my hands with soap vs. wiping them down with just a Wet Nap; and I was able to look in the mirror at my highly unattractive but, at the same time, excusable hairstyle. I promised myself to not take for granted the ability to sit upright again, ever.

———

At the end of the week, which felt like a month, I was sitting up for 90 minutes at a time and was finally being discharged. The return of my privacy, freedom to move around outside of that bathroom-sized room, and a solid night's sleep are a few from the top of my list of things I was looking forward to most in my discharge. I knew I'd kind of miss the food, though, and the excuse to not shave my armpits.

I haven't talked about this yet.

Disregarding for a minute my desire to be ladylike and attract a forever-man, I'll share that my armpit hair grew beautifully long during those weeks. At one point Casey, one of my favorite nurses, offered to bring me a razor, but I said I don't want "that thing anywhere near me." I was joking, but also kind of serious. She also offered to shave my legs, but I think she was just being nice—that hair grows blonde.

In that month, my armpit hair grew long enough for me to know that I won't ever stop shaving them because, had I let it go much longer, it would be itchy and an uncomfortable situation for everyone. More power to you, female hipsters that keep long hair under your arms. I tried it, but it's just not for me.

———

"Are you ready to leave?" Mom asked. Somehow, between things sent from friends at home and Mom and Dad's regular offers of "requests from the store," I accumulated stuff, a lot of stuff. She already made one trip to the car and had her hands full of more.

"I'm ready." I looked around the small room for the last time, God willing. "Let's get out of here."

"Bye sweetie," a familiar woman said from the threshold of my hospital room. "I hope to never see you again."

Now I know she meant that as "I hope I'll never see you again in the context of this hospital because I care about your well-being," but it still feels like a rude choice of words. So, I gave it right back to her.

"Yes," I said. "I hope I'll never see you again, either."

That's called passive aggression and I am very good at it.

She smiled broadly and we shuffled past her toward the exit door. Dad and Achilles were outside waiting for us in his [very tall] truck. Nothing could have made me happier in that moment.

"You're free," Dad said, exclaimed, and got out of the truck to meet us. "Let's get out of here."

He took my cell phone from my lap, put it in a pocket in the truck's door, then lifted me into the passenger seat. The three of us, four if you're counting Ms. Achilles, buckled in. I hadn't stopped smiling yet.

––––––––

"Before I shave my armpits, will you braid the hair for me?" I asked Mom once we were on the road back to our condo. She was sitting behind me in the car and Dad was driving next to me. I barely heard his gasp. He looked over at me and I lifted my arm in the air. We both saw that yes, in fact, my hair was long enough to braid.

"Whatever you want, sweetie," she said. "Today is your day."

––––––––

I'm kidding about that last part; my armpit hair wasn't long enough to braid. Replace "braid my hair" with "go to Target and get sushi for lunch," though, and that's the truth.

Mom, Dad, and I drove away from Promise Hospital with a back seat full of dead flowers, cards, balloons, and grocery store requests. I was sitting in a car and choosing what I wanted to eat for lunch and, on the long days lying in a bed at Promise, those are things I felt I would never do again.

The inevitability of being admitted to a hospital isn't something I would wish on anyone, ever, but the humility of the situation resulted in my appreciation for the small and beautiful parts of life. The small things, like shaving my armpits.

Two Minutes

There are a lot of setbacks that come with my disability, but there's an avalanche of good things, great things, that come with it, too. I've talked a lot about the struggle of dating with a disability in my other book, but those struggles are very real and ever-evolving. My wheelchair is a little bit of a stick in the mud in regard to my physical attraction and that, no surprise, has stood in the way of what I thought were many opportunities with good men.

But, when it comes to dating and love, Greater Things came.

———

My church is one of the happiest and most fun places in my life. The people remember your name, the celebrations are loud and often include dessert food, and the energy is overflowing.

My faith in God has definitely ridden a rollercoaster throughout my life, but there has always been a foundation. When I started going to Hill City Church, my coaster started, and has remained, going uphill.

One thing you should note here: I'm a creature of habit. Every Sunday I attend the 8 AM service, every Sunday I sit in the same seat, and every Sunday I park in the same spot. This particular Sunday, though, I slept through my alarm and missed the early service; I went to the 9:30 service.

When I was rolling to my spot in the second row of the middle section, I saw that someone, a boy, was sitting in my seat. I rolled closer and realized that, in fact, it was not a boy in my spot. It was a man, a very attractive man.

"Hi," I said. "This is my seat. Who are you?"

That's how I thought I started the conversation, but he's since told me that he didn't know it was "my" seat until later on. Thank God for some manners.

It probably went something like:

"Hi, I'm Kristin. Good morning."

"Nice to meet you. I'm Chris."

We had a couple minutes of small talk before church started, then I parked my wheelchair in front of him, in the front row. Before I turned around, he recalls, I said "Don't go anywhere. I'll talk to you at Two Minutes to Talk."

To me that just sounds bossy but, when Chris tells the story, he says he was "overjoyed."

Two Minutes to Talk is a time after the announcements where we're given a prompt and two minutes to meet people around us. The prompt that Sunday was "What's something you want to be better at?" and, for whatever reason, I turned around and talked to Chris for two minutes about how bad of an eater I am and how I'd like to be better at cooking. I detailed to him, this attractive stranger, that I have a beautiful kitchen in my home and access to nutritious food, but I don't use the kitchen and I survive on tortilla chips alone. The word "malnourished" might even have come up.

In hindsight, not the best first impression to make; everyone can agree that talking about my flaws for two solid minutes should erase all of the appeal I had just established. I reflected on our conversation on the way home and reasoned that, because he's an attractive man sitting alone at church, he's likely married, engaged, or in a serious relationship, so it didn't matter what I said. Call me a pessimist or just burned too many times, but I had little faith that a quality, single man can be found in the church.

Thank God he's persistent.

I was out of town the next two weeks, didn't see him again and, honestly, forgot completely about him. When I returned home, it was time to sign up for small groups, which are Bible study groups led by church members. I lead a small group out of my home so, as orchestrated by God himself, Chris saw my name on a list and it happened to be the only one that worked into his schedule.

In a better way than I could have planned, Chris came to my house for the first meeting of our small group, asked me on a date the following Saturday, and I agreed. I was signed up for a pottery class that morning and, in an effort to protect my heart from being hurt by yet another man, I kept my figurative distance; instead of getting overly excited and canceling my plans to accommodate the date, I invited him to join me at the pottery class. I was playing it cool, or at least trying to.

Saturday morning came, I made a plate shaped like a mouth and he made a fish figurine, then we went to a street festival outside the studio. At that point I liked him pretty well, but I was in my creative element, so it's hard to judge whether I was into him, or just very happy about crafts and a festival.

The festival turned out boring, so we didn't stay long. Instead, we came back to my house and took a three-mile walk around my neighborhood.

"This is the most creative I've ever been," he said after the pottery class. Then, after the walk, "this is the most active I've been in a long time." I, being a very creative and very athletic person, heard that and thought "uh oh."

After the walk, we went to dinner at a taco restaurant in the city, then to a brewery to meet up with a group of his friends. I don't even remotely enjoy the taste of beer, but that night at the brewery is where I finished my first entire glass. Call that being caught up in the moment, or trying to fit in with his friends, but it did nothing to change my opinions. I still don't like the taste of beer.

In fact, that day was another first for me: the first date I've been on that lasted more than 11 hours.

From there on, Chris routinely came to small group at my house, we started sitting next to each other at Sunday church services (I got my seat back), and we continued to date each other. A little more than one month later, we exchanged "I love you"s after a night of dancing at the wedding of his best friends, two of the people I met at the brewery on our first date. The rest is history, in the making.

————

When talking about dating, people have always said two things: "when you know, you know" and "it'll happen when you least expect it." I'm tellin' ya: I wanted to roll over their toes every time they said either one. My response? "Yes, but I've *known* with every boy I've dated," and "I haven't *expected* anything for years."

But then I met Chris, and I *knew.* I met him on a morning I slept through my alarm, slapped on the first t-shirt in my reach, had my hair in a sloppy bun, and was *definitely* not expecting it. But, when I met him, I just *knew.* Please realize how annoying it is that those people and those sayings were right.

The difference, I realize, between my relationship with Chris and that of my ex-boyfriends is that God is, has always been, at the center. I've heard people say that "a man should have to seek God in order to find his way to you," and I've rolled my eyes in the same way at that saying than I did at the others; that one felt like a fantasy just as much as *knowing* felt like a fantasy.

Once again, the people were right.

Putting God in the center of our relationship looks like: accountability in our perspectives and attendance of church; mature conversations and character; confidence in our communication; and an understanding that we are second.

Thinking back and reading these stories, I see my desire and pursuit of companionship laced throughout. Although it's not a main theme, I manage to identify and pursue an attractive man, usually only in my mind, in nearly every instance. Good looking men are a great way to keep me interested and entertained during an activity, but now I have the discernment to see they were all miscalculations.

Make no mistake: they're probably beautiful people with great personalities, but the feelings I felt weren't even in the same ballpark as when I *know*. Take my experience and my advice as something to give you hope. It's not just something people say because it sounds good:

Love will come to you when you least expect it—even when you're wearing a t-shirt and a sloppy bun. And you're going to *know*.

The Light

In August of 2005, doctors looked at me and said, among a long list of predictions, that I'll never be able to feel or move below my belly button again. They said my life will never look the same, but they didn't give me the complete picture.

Things will never be the same, they were right about that, but that doesn't mean my life can't be very good. There has been and will continue to be struggle, broken friendships, and lots of inequality, but those are on an equally long list of things I can overcome. Paralysis is not my end game and there is hope for my healing. This disability is just as much mental as it is physical, though, so I've had to rest a lot of my belief in my body and mind to heal themselves.

There's a lot of loss and bad things laced into my story of disability, but there are even more good things. Sure, I lost ease of mobility throughout the world and I've struggled a lot with skin breakdown, but the people I've met, places I've traveled, and opportunities that have opened up have made the setbacks that come with my disability worth the trouble. My accident, with its ongoing challenges, required my family to come together and function as a team. My close relationship with my parents facilitated my living with them until I was able to save money and build my first home. Some things still brought difficulty and I've had trouble fitting in on numerous occasions, but I think that's just how growing up works. As for me, I have very few things to complain about.

I still have my mind and I still have the means to find the positive parts in this, and I've learned I have to take the time to find that perspective. With that peace of mind, I see that there really are so many other things worse than what I deal with; physical setbacks are surmountable.

In a lot of ways, this disability has kicked my butt; not many, but a few times I've been tempted to relax into it and accept it as my permanent. But I can't do that, I can't give up on myself. My doctors told me there's no hope for my recovery, but I've proven them wrong so, so many times already. Nothing about the human body is permanent and there's no reason I can't overcome this, both mentally and physically. I've had to relearn and reprioritize every aspect of my life, but that's what it takes to fight this fight. I've rooted myself in God, who is consistent and gives me hope to change my circumstance. As long as I go into the fight with a positive attitude and a stubborn head, I can live a full and happy life, regardless of my inabilities.

And so, my journey continues.

About the Author

 Kristin Beale is a native of Richmond, Virginia. She is the author of a book, *Greater Things*, and a comic book, *Date Me*. She's a regular contributor to the Christopher and Dana Reeve Foundation's blog, and she publishes a comic every week on Instagram at @greater. things.comics. Kristin is an 8-time marathon finisher, parafencer, and mother to a beautiful dog named Achilles Jones.

CPSIA information can be obtained
at www.ICGtesting.com
Printed in the USA
JSHW041359161220
10310JS00001B/45

9 781631 950704